# AMC Field Guide to Trail Building and Maintenance

## 2nd Edition

# AMC Field Guide to Trail Building and Maintenance

## 2nd Edition

**Robert D. Proudman
and Reuben Rajala**

Appalachian Mountain Club

In association with the
National Park Service, National Trails Program

SECOND EDITION

ISBN 0-910146-30-6

© 1981 by Appalachian Mountain Club

The paper used in this publication meets the minimum requirements of the American National Standard for Information Sciences—Permanence of Paper for Printed Library Materials, ANSI Z39.48-1984.∞™

Printed in the United States of America

# CONTENTS

# PUBLISHER'S PREFACE

THE TRAIL — IT'S SOMETHING hikers, campers, cross-country skiers, and other users may not think much about, may perhaps even take for granted. That is, until it is lost through improper marking, or until it becomes a mosquito-infested swamp through poor drainage. Then, and perhaps only then, do we realize that the trail is the essential medium without which many of our sports would be impossible. A change seems to be in the wind, though. The hiker and his trails are becoming important considerations in outdoor recreation and backcountry management.

The Appalachian Mountain Club has been interested in trails longer than most organizations. The Club's trail crew program is over half a century old. Its budget has increased tenfold since the sixties, and new initiatives have been made to involve staff and volunteers in the many facets of trail work.

A recent Neilsen poll listed camping as the fourth largest participant sport in America, with 58.1 million people involved. Camping is also among the ten fastest growing participant sports, registering a 7% growth rate between 1973 and 1976. Other outdoor sports that impact on trails, although less directly than camping, are also among the 25 largest participant sports: bicycling, hunting, fishing, skiing, snowmobiling, and motorcycling.

With the increased interest in trails nationally, the AMC's long years of experience and the many dollars spent are suddenly starting to be recognized, not only in the Club's traditional White Mountain domain, but in other areas around the country, and even internationally.

This book is the distillation of that expertise. First assembled by Robert D. Proudman, formerly the AMC's trails supervisor, it covers all the skills and equipment needed to plan, build, and maintain trails. The second edition, updated principally by current AMC trails supervisor Reuben Rajala, expands upon the information provided in the earlier book, based on experience gained and comments received since then. The book is intended for anyone, anywhere in the world, who is responsible for trail activities — government agencies, outing clubs, hiking groups, ski touring centers, and nonprofit organizations involved in outdoor recreation and backcountry management. It is also for trail users. Each of us who spends time on the trail should understand how fragile it is, and how much work goes into its care and feeding. Only then will we respect it properly. And perhaps only then will we be willing to work to save that endangered species — the trail.

# ACKNOWLEDGMENTS

THIS BOOK HAS TRULY BEEN A COOPERATIVE effort by volunteers, members, and staff of the Appalachian Mountain Club (AMC), as well as by outside groups. Countless individuals and organizations have made contributions.

The current AMC trail crew deserves the credit for developing or adapting from outside sources the techniques described here. Past trailmasters, crew leaders, and members have also contributed in a dynamic way to the evolution of the concepts now being used in trail design, building, and maintenance.

This book could not have been done without the leadership, encouragement, and dynamic example set by J. Joseph May, AMC trails supervisor from 1961 to 1971. Joe made possible a climate where crew members were encouraged to think and to employ new ideas and concepts to manage the problems that had to be faced on trails.

This, in turn, could not have taken place without the trust and good will of the Appalachian Mountain Club. The AMC executive staff, Trails Committee, and Executive Council have permitted experimentation and have prodded for positive results through investment of Club funds in the trails program.

Reuben Rajala, as AMC trails coordinator several years ago and more recently as AMC trails supervisor, donated many hours to review all sections of this book. He also wrote parts of the first draft of the trail reconstruction and tool sections, as well as updating the second edition and adding the new chapters on trail inventories, bridges, stiles, and ski touring trails. Sally Surgenor, at the time AMC research assistant, wrote the first draft of the section on soils. Ed Spencer, then AMC research director, wrote the section on vegetation, as well as parts of the reconstruction chapter. Roger Moore, the current AMC trails coordinator, and Tim Davis, while working for the Club on a special trails project, reviewed and contributed to the second edition.

Artists Marc Lacroix and Jean Farquhar sketched several drafts of each drawing and completed a demanding agenda of art work. Janis Merkle and Marina Weinquist also contributed drawings. George Bellerose and Cindy Robinson provided most of the fine photographs that illustrate the book. Reuben Rajala and Nate Mulherin also contributed photos.

Members of the trail crew who helped write and review much of the first edition section on reconstruction include Steve Rice, Jon Vara, Bruce Davis, Jon Coe, and Bill Birchard. Many unnamed crew members laid down their hand tools and took pen in hand to convey their working techniques.

Much of the information on signs was provided by our sign maker for many years, the late Clyde Smith. Clyde's craftsmanship is visible in many signs up and down the Appalachian Trail.

Other information came from Bruce Davis, the Club's present sign maker, and Lester Kenway of the Maine Appalachian Trail Club.

The Forest Service, U. S. Department of Agriculture (USDA), helped directly through staff assistance, particularly from Ray Leonard at the USDA Northeast Forest Station, as well as indirectly through their publications and bulletins. Staff members of the White Mountain National Forest have contributed information and expertise in their steward's role as managers of the national forest that contains most of the AMC's trail system.

The Appalachian Trail Conference, through its volunteers, staff, and publications, has contributed, as has the Society for the Protection of New Hampshire Forests, whose help made possible the section on private land.

The AMC Publications Department provided professional guidance, especially in final drafts and production of the first edition. The second edition was edited by Arlyn Powell and produced by Michael Cirone, Betsey Tryon and Sally Carrel. The AMC Department of Financial Resources, under the direction of Sam Rogers, wrote proposals that led to funding of the original manuscript.

The Howard and Bush Foundation in Hartford, Connecticut showed exemplary confidence and foresight in funding an unfinished manuscript.

Tom Deans, AMC executive director, deserves credit for his trust, guidance, and enforcement of unpleasant but nonetheless essential deadlines.

And finally, and in a practical sense most important, much credit goes to Kim Smith, my secretary, and the office staff at Pinkham Notch Camp for their prompt and cheerful typing, copying, and editing of countless drafts of this book.

*Robert D. Proudman*
*Spring, 1981*

# INTRODUCTION

THE APPALACHIAN MOUNTAIN CLUB has for many years been a moving force behind hiking programs in the northeastern United States. Club officers and members have actively mapped, designed, and built many of the hiking trails that exist in this area today, providing access into its most beautiful backcountry.

In 1920 Club officers instituted a professional trail crew, the first of its kind in the country. This crew was based in the White Mountains of New Hampshire, where it developed and maintained trails primarily for Club members and programs. Today the crew consists of thirty seasonal employees and two full-time staff members who are responsible for approximately 600 miles of hiking trails, including about 120 miles of the Appalachian National Scenic Trail, 20 miles of ski touring trail, and 20 shelters and tentsites in the White Mountain region.

Beginning in the early 1960's increased public use of backcountry facilities became apparent. Tabulations made at more popular campsites since 1970 have shown an average increase in the use of White Mountain trails of 10-15% per year. The AMC trail crew has grown to meet the greater needs that have been developing with this increasing public use.

The Club's trails budget in 1965 was $10,000; in 1975 it was $100,000. Most of the funds are still derived from membership dues and donations. Cooperative funding for specific projects and programs has at times been arranged with various federal agencies. A new booster program allows hikers to donate toward a specific trail project each year and receive lapel pins identifying them as supporters.

The programs financed by the Club's trails budget have grown in complexity as well as size. Today both volunteers and staff are involved in this work. Supplementing the Club's paid trail crew members and shelter caretakers are forty to fifty annual participants in a one-week volunteer trail crew and many more participants in a new volunteer Adopt-A-Trail program, where basic trail maintenance is done at the volunteer's own pace and on his own time.

Additionally, the AMC's ten chapters and seven major camps, spread from Maine through the Delaware Valley of Pennsylvania, are involved in local trail work. Each chapter has a Trails Committee, and a Clubwide Trails Committee of volunteers sets policy and oversees the work of the Club professionals.

The historical function of the Club's professional crew was for years simply to clear brush and keep trails marked. There are stories of how the crew visited roadside campgrounds to solicit hikers to tramp down the trails and so to help keep them open. The situation today is considerably different. Unprecedented numbers of visitors have taxed the physical ability of soils and plant life to remain healthy and stable under the pressure of great volumes of traffic. Aggravated erosion on slopes is rampant on many mountain trails. Sanitation problems and litter disposal have degraded the areas used for overnight camping.

AMC volunteers, staff, and trail crews have developed programs and techniques to meet these new demands. This book is an effort to distill and describe the best of the knowledge that is currently available. It also draws upon experience and techniques distilled from other trail manuals and gathered from correspondence and discussions with those involved in trail work around the U.S. and beyond. These techniques are applicable to some degree to all foot trails, so they can be employed and further adapted to solve similar trail problems in other popular mountain areas. All techniques described have been developed through the trial and error of practical application in the field.

Coupled with the need to improve environmental trail management at popular facilities in our mountain parks and forests is a growing need to implement trail programs to build new trails and to protect existing trails on the local, town, and county levels. Second home development and competing trail use from off-road vehicles have forced some trails to close. Trail development on privately owned local property provides recreational opportunities nearer to home. Town, county, and state parks are more available if access is eased using trail development. Residents can then gain local recreational opportunities normally reserved for vacation times and for places removed from their day-to-day community environment.

The trails program of the Appalachian Mountain Club exemplifies the advantages of private, charitable, and nonprofit development, maintenance, and management of public recreational facilities and programs. Such programs can greatly complement traditional state and federal trail programs.

It is our hope that in publishing this book we can stimulate similar private trail groups, outing clubs, community groups, and interested individuals to take a more active part in trail development, maintenance, and protection. There is common cause to unify and develop a national program to protect the rights of our citizens to travel on foot through natural settings, unfettered in the pursuit of this most fundamental recreational activity.

# 1

# DESIGNING TRAILS

---

*The job of recreational engineering is not one of building trails into lovely country, but of building receptivity into the yet unloving human mind.*

*Aldo Leopold*

TRAILS DESIGNED AND MAINTAINED so that they provide satisfying recreational access into natural areas with minimum impact are the primary goal of the techniques in this book. Review of some basic guidelines for locating and maintaining trails will ensure that the resulting facilities can provide opportunities for meeting the recreational needs of hikers.

The trail should blend into the natural surroundings by maintaining continuity and regularity in the way it traverses land. Sudden changes in direction or too much meandering should be avoided. Likewise, long, straight sections should be used temperately; they lack interest for hikers.

There should be regularity in clearing and marking throughout the trail's length. For example, changing the way a trail is marked midway along its length will cause hikers confusion. This also applies to trails that are climbing a slope. Hikers using such trails should not have to lose significant elevation unnecessarily because of poor design. The trail should be consistent in climbing into the high country if this is its function.

Cultural and historic features such as old dam and mill sites, cellar holes, and old village sites can add historical and educational dimensions to a trail design. Research into an area's cultural features should be done in order to optimize the value of a trail's location. Interpretive information in guidebooks and on signs can make this information available to walkers.

In some cases the reputation of a feature, be it a natural one such as a mountain summit or a manmade one such as a village site or an old mine, may be great enough to attract use even though trail access does not exist. In these cases it may be advisable to install a trail in order to contain traffic on a well-planned route. Several trailless summits in the Adirondacks of New York have been damaged because hikers have visited these summits by bushwhacking or using "bootleg" trails. An excessive number of unplanned trails approach these summits like the spokes of a wheel approaching the hub. If a well-designed trail provides access, damage from trampling to these sensitive alpine summits can be reduced.

One of the greatest highlights a trail can offer is the scenic vista. The traveler should have the feeling that, for the most part, the land mass is below him at such vistas.

All trails have terminuses, which are respectively the *trailhead* or start of the trail (usually located at roadside) and the *destination,* be it a mountain summit, waterfall, mill site, or similar feature. Destinations in a system of trails will, for any single trail, include other trails and campsites.

The choice of route, in addition to connecting these termi-nuses and maintaining regular marking standards, slope, and direction, should incorporate beautiful and dramatic natural features. Diverse biological, climatic, and topographical char-acteristics should be condensed into short sections of trail wherever possible. Outlooks, rock outcrops, stream sides, and similar features of the landscape please the traveler and there-fore should be integrated into the trail location. High-quality trail design is primarily a balance between beauty and function. Natural features and scenery exist ideally in creative juxtaposi-tion with the continuity, efficiency, and durability of a proposed route.

## Anatomy of a Trail

A trail is made up of components, the sum of which make up the total view of the trail environment seen by the hiker. The following is a description of these components — what they are and how they complement each other in the design of a trail. Defining these terms now will assist in understanding subse-quent chapters.

The *trail treadway* or *trail tread* is the surface upon which the hiker makes direct contact with the soil. It is the location for virtually all improvements that ease hiker passage by hardening and stabilizing soils from shifting, eroding, or becoming muddy. Popular trails will damage soils on slopes and in wet terrain; therefore, good maintenance of the treadway occasion-ally requires reconstruction and rehabilitation of the original soil profile. The treadway is the most important component of any foot trail.

The trail *right-of-way* is the area around the treadway that is cleared for passage of the hiker. It is usually four to six feet wide, depending on vegetation density. The term "right-of-way'' also refers to legal right of passage, such as would be the case with a protected trail on private land.

The *trail corridor*[1] includes the treadway, right-of-way, and all the lands that make up the environment of the trail as viewed by the hiker. The Forest Service calls it the ''zone of travel influence.'' This terminology shows that the corridor includes all those lands having an influence on the hiker's perception of the trail environment.

In particularly important trail systems, such as the Appalachian National Scenic Trail, this corridor takes on added importance. Legislation passed by the U.S. Congress requires that the corridor of the Appalachian Trail be protected from adverse developments that would be detrimental to its natural quality. However, such acquisition is an expensive and difficult proposition. Therefore, definition of the corridor's width takes on

[1]This material has been developed with reference to *Guidelines for the Appalachian Trail*, U.S. Department of the Interior, 1971.

critical importance. In some situations state and federal plans have defined the Appalachian Trail corridor as being two hundred feet wide, even though in open forests, on lake shores, and above treeline this obviously does not include all the lands that influence the hiker. Managers of the Appalachian Trail are presently trying to define this corridor more accurately, in order to effectively protect the quality of the experience of walking along it.

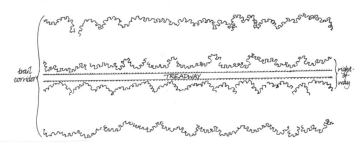

The *buffer* or *protection zone* is the land area on each side of the trail treadway. The buffer zones, along with the treadway and the right-of-way, make up the total trail corridor. Buffer zones are the areas that insulate the hiker from activities detrimental to the hiking experience, such as second home development, mining, or logging.

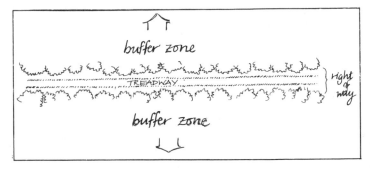

Buffers can also be used to protect particularly fragile areas from damage due to hikers. Trail layout around sensitive plant life, lake shores, and springs should include buffers to protect these fragile areas from trampling.

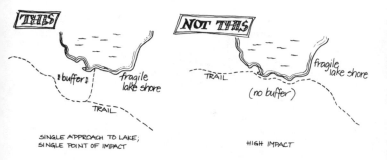

SINGLE APPROACH TO LAKE;
SINGLE POINT OF IMPACT                                    HIGH IMPACT

## Formats for Trail System Design

There are three major formats that can be used in trail design.

The *loop* is a popular format for day-use trails because it enables easy access and parking. Hikers do not have to return on the same trail; therefore, interest and satisfaction in hiking a loop can be kept at a high level.

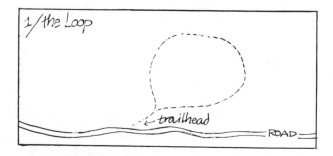

The *horseshoe* can be a valuable trail format, especially in areas where public transportation is available. It can also be used as an appropriate alternative to auto travel on roads where distances between terminuses are not too great. Ski touring trail development in the Mt. Washington Valley of New Hampshire has trailheads at inns and restaurants in the valley connected by trails in the horseshoe format. Many hiking trails are of this type.

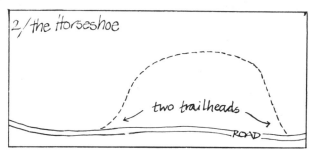

The *line* is the simplest and most common format for trails. It connects two points — e.g., the roadside trailhead and the destination, which may be a summit, waterfall, or similar feature. A good example of trails in the line format are firewarden's trails to lookout towers on mountain summits. Long-distance trails such as the Appalachian Trail and Pacific Crest Trail are

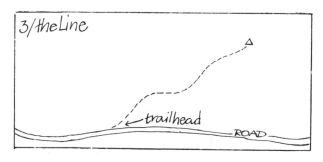

premiere examples of trails in the line format. These "trunk
line" trails on public lands with high scenic value are aug-
mented with side trails, alternate routes, and connectors to form
trail systems.

A *trail system* should use these different formats to satisfy a
diversity of recreational needs. Careful design will provide
trails for different users with different expectations. Multi-day
backpackers as well as day hikers can be served by a well-
designed trail system.

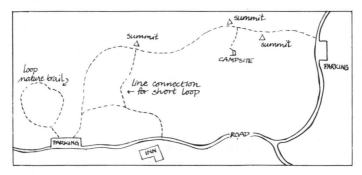

## Trail Access

The type and volume of public access to a proposed trail is a
powerful factor that needs to be studied carefully in its design. If
a trailhead is proposed on a major recreational highway, then
one may accurately forecast that visitor use will be high; therefore, for safety and to protect the resources of the proposed trail
corridor, the standards of the trail must be correspondingly
higher. This requirement for high standards means that planning
must be more comprehensive and that the investment in design
and construction must be substantial if the trail is to be safe,
enjoyable, and environmentally stable. The reverse is also true:

if access is from an infrequently used rural road, then the standard of the proposed trail can be reduced and the cost and effort in planning, design, and construction can be correspondingly lower.

The location and size of parking facilities allow a degree of use control. If the designer wants a reduced volume of use, then parking should be nonexistent or limited. If parking is plentiful and accessible, use may tend to increase, increasing the maintenance needs of the trail.

For reasons of safety, the location of parking facilities on highways must be carefully planned. Efforts at design and maintenance of parking facilities should be coordinated with the appropriate representatives of the state Highway Department or Department of Transportation. Their specifications for the location of a parking facility on a highway should, in large part, determine the location of the trailhead.

Parking facilities should also be coordinated with other recreational uses. If a picnic area already exists, then placing the trailhead in this locale will obviously preclude the need for a new parking lot. If a snowmobile trail has parking available, then a summer hiking trail placed in the same vicinity will reduce the cost of building additional facilities.

Management of trailhead parking may additionally require that there be litter collection facilities, signs, and information boards. These needs should be planned into a trail design so that no problems exist after installation.

A recreational trail should buffer the hiker from the sight of and noise from manmade features such as roads, railroad tracks, logging operations, and second home development. In cases where the trail must cross a road, railroad, logging operation, or similar feature, the designer should place the trail so as to minimize the hiker's exposure to these debilitating characteristics. These areas should be crossed in the shortest practical manner, usually at right angles. Long lines of sight should be avoided to keep conflicts with landowners to a minimum.

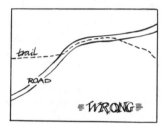 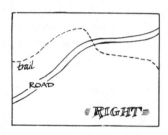

In addition to minimizing the negative experiential impact of road and railroad crossings, right angle crossings are also safer.

All of these general concepts should be refined to suit specific needs for the planning and design or maintenance of any particular trail. Any trail project, in order to be efficiently executed with high-quality results, should be thought through with proper consideration for the primary objective of meeting the recreational needs of hikers.

**2**

# ENVIRONMENTAL CONSIDERATIONS IN TRAIL DESIGN

ENVIRONMENTAL DESIGN OF TRAILS requires that the designer pay close attention to the soil characteristics of the area in question. This chapter will give the reader a broad overview of soils and their characteristics, especially when subject to trampling from hiking.

## Soil Characteristics

*Soil* is a mixture of organic matter, water, mineral matter, and air; it comprises the root zone of living plants. Soil covers most of the surface of the earth and varies in thickness from inches to hundreds of feet. This covering of soil is like a mosaic, with different soil types and characteristics distinguishable from place to place. Each soil is composed of one or more *layers* or *horizons* that, when looked at as a unit, can be called the *soil profile*.

There are several ways in which soil fails to support hiking use.

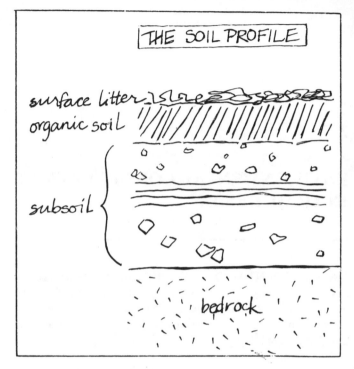

**Compaction** — Hiking causes plants to bend, break, and eventually die. After this mortality, the surface horizons of soil compact into a cement-like hardness. This compacted surface loses its pore space and, therefore, its ability to absorb surface water. If this water is not absorbed into the compacted soil it will puddle on the trail, or if on a slope, will start to flow downhill causing erosion. Research has shown that a stream of water will flow up to fifteen times farther on compacted soil than on soil in its naturally porous condition.[1]

---

[1]Winklaar, Paul, *Forest Road Location on Northern New Hampshire Soils*, Cooperative Extension Service, University of New Hampshire, Durham, August, 1971, p. 7.

**Surface Erosion** — Erosion is a natural process in which soils are worn away by the action of wind, water, glaciers, and other natural phenomena. On trails this natural process is aggravated by soil compaction and the almost constant churning agitation of hiking traffic. Water flowing over the compacted soil surface detaches the smaller, lighter soil particles and carries them downhill. The greater the velocity of flowing water, the greater the mass of soil that can be carried. Velocity is increased as slope steepens. Increased volume of water runoff also increases velocity. At high elevations, greater amounts of water accumulate than in neighboring valleys. Ecological studies carried out in Vermont for six years have shown that greater amounts of rainfall occur at a 3600-foot elevation than at 1800 feet.

In addition to direct precipitation, the needles of spruce and fir trees, which dominate the landscape at high elevations, "comb" water from clouds.

These large volumes of water, made more damaging by steep slopes and foot traffic, create a particularly serious erosion hazard on trails in mountain areas. This erosion can quickly destroy a trail treadway. Research done in the Adirondacks indicates a soil loss of one inch per year on some hiking trails.[2] Layout, soils, and use are all important factors.

A treadway in the early stages of being eroded is easy to spot. Loose stones and gravel are left after the smaller, stabilizing sand and silt particles have been removed by water. These stones make for poor footing, which in turn causes the hiker to walk on the edge of the trail, thereby killing plants, compacting

---

[2] Ketchledge, E.H., and Leonard, R.E., "The Impact of Man on the Adirondack High Country," *The New York Conservationist*, October-November, 1970, pp. 14-18.

the soil, and generally initiating a vicious circle of plant mortality, compaction, and erosion that will eventually change a trail into a boulder-strewn gully.

FROM THIS......                TO THIS

Erosion, in addition to causing uncertain footing and unsightly gullies, can cause resource damage beyond the trail's treadway. After sediment-loaded water slows down, soil particles are deposited on the forest floor, suffocating smaller plant life — and in serious situations even suffocating trees by covering up the lower trunks. If these sediments find their way into streams and ponds they can kill fish and, by adding solid nutrients to water, accelerate the eutrophication of waterways. Soil loss around the base of trees can expose roots to disease and weaken their anchoring function, allowing trees to blow down much more easily. Also, an eroded, rough trail may result in hikers walking to either side of the trail, further aggravating soil and plant disturbance.

Because of the possibilities for resource degradation, trail design, installation, and maintenance in mountainous backcountry must employ a careful evaluation of soil characteristics in order to be successful. Wherever possible, trails should be located on soils that are capable of withstanding the amount of use anticipated without eroding or becoming wet and muddy.

This ability of soil to withstand traffic of a given intensity depends on several factors. In some cases a single factor can be limiting, so that soil will degrade swiftly despite other more enduring qualities it may possess. In other cases a combination of factors are important to consider in determining the best location for the trail. These factors are soil wetness, texture, structure, and depth.

*Soil Wetness* — Soil wetness may be caused by poor drainage. *Ground water* moving through the landscape may saturate the surface of soils, especially during periods of heavy rainfall and the spring thaw. The level of ground water is called the *water table*. It fluctuates with the wetness of the season. The *seasonally high water table* is the highest level of ground water during the wettest month of the year. This seasonally high water table in shallow or poorly drained soils will create surface springs and seeps which can create problems on a compacted treadway. In very poorly drained soils, such as in bogs or depressions near lakes and streams, water moves so slowly that the soil surface may be wet for much of the year. Trails in such areas should be avoided.

*Soil Wetness Indicators* — There are several indicators that can be used to evaluate soil wetness in the field. The most obvious and simple evaluation is visiting the site during periods of high water run off — after long periods of rainfall or during the spring snow melt. If much surface water is evident in many rivulets, then the site is limited in its appropriateness for trail location. Dig a shallow hole along the proposed trail site; if it fills with water or if water placed in it does not percolate down and out of the hole, then there is either a high water table or drainage is inhibited. In both cases trail use will degrade the environment.

The color of subsurface soils can be a practical clue to drainage conditions. Most soils contain some iron compounds which, if alternately exposed to air and water, oxidize to take on a reddish-brown color. Soils with these colors present can therefore indicate free movement of air and water as conditions of wetness change. It is likely that such soils are well drained and therefore appropriate for trail use if other conditions are not limiting.

An additional indication of good drainage is the uniformity of the soil's coloring. Uniform coloring can indicate free air and water movement through the soil. Correspondingly, "mottles" of red or yellow imposed on a uniform background indicate short periods of poor drainage, perhaps in the spring. Mottling or layering of gray or bluish-gray soil indicates longer or perennially poor drainage. In areas where dark organic soils predominate these mottles may be "masked" and unrecognizable, but they can still be there.

Soils that have a thick, dark brown or black surface horizon may also drain poorly. Some of these soils are called *peats* or *mucks*. They are usually located in bogs, depressions, and areas of poor drainage. These fragile soils are poor for trail locations unless a bridge boardwalk is provided to keep hikers out of direct contact with them.

*Soil Texture* — Soil texture refers to the relative proportions of various sized groups of grains in a mass of soil. It is an important characteristic in the trafficability of soils. In general, loam soils with a mixture of sands, clay, and silt will resist compaction and erosion most successfully. The smaller sizes of silt and clay particles add cohesion; sand and gravel are present for porosity and water absorption. These moderately sandy soils will resist compaction and will absorb a high level of rainfall, making them good for trail use.

Caution should be used when building trails across pure sand. Sand blows when dry, supports few plants for soil retention, and can lead to a shifting treadway.

Soils made up mostly of silt and clay will be muddy when wet, cracked and dusty when dry. These soils are highly erodible and if possible should be avoided for trails, especially on steep slopes. Coarse fragments in the treadway can increase trafficability. Gravel-sized fragments imbedded in the soil matrix help to hold the more erodible sand, silt, and clay particles in place. They also improve soil drainage. Loose gravel on the trail surface may cause uncertain footing, but this is not a serious limitation for a trail.

Rocks and stones, while making footing somewhat variable, are not serious limitations to trail placement either. In fact, they can be natural erosion retardants when used in a trail treadway.

Field inspection of soil texture can easily be done by feeling with the fingers. Sometimes this process is supplemented with a hand lens. Here is what to look for:

*Sand* — Loose, single grains; individual grains readily seen and easily felt.

*Loam* — A mixture of different grades of sand, silt, and clay; it has a gritty feel, yet is fairly smooth and plastic.

*Clay* — A fine-textured soil which usually breaks into clods or lumps that are hard when dry; quite plastic and sticky when wet.

*Soil Structure* — The relationships between horizons and the characteristics of each horizon affect the percolation of water into soils. Many soils have hard, compacted horizons called *hardpans*. These hardpans are generally impervious to the downward movement of water. In areas where hardpans are evident, trail surfaces may become wet and soft, making them susceptible to damage.

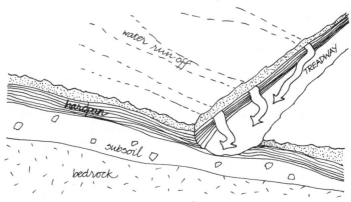

*Soil Depth* — Shallow soils over bedrock or hardpan can lead to problems on hiking trails. Such soils are often heavy and saturated with water, causing them to erode quickly and slough off when walked upon. This is especially true in steep terrain, where steep rock slabs can become dangerously exposed after some wear from hiking. Hikers seeking safe passage use plant life on the edge of the trail for handholds, killing the plants and aggravating trail widening problems. This process is, in most cases, unsuitable to enjoyable hiking and disruptive to the natural environment.

The limitations of soil depth are especially critical in the alpine zone. The soil mantle here is only several inches thick and plant life is small and easily damaged by foot traffic. In the alpine zone the maintainer must take special pains to mark the trail without any abrupt turns. In this way shortcuts are discouraged. Lining the path with rock, and in extreme cases even rock wall, will help to contain the impact of hiking traffic on thin alpine soils to a small area.

Soil depth and grade are the most important factors in determining the appropriateness of trail location. They are both easy to measure in the field with a soil auger, by eye, or with an inclinometer. Therefore, they can usually be evaluated during the initial phases of a proposed trail installation.

## Topography

Topographical variations[3] in the landscape such as hills, knolls, and views are elements of a stimulating and interesting trail design. If the trail fits the lay of the land, hikers will have a greater sense of adventure and anticipation in traveling. Subtle turns and undulations in grade, steep and dramatic climbs to a view, or the sudden appearance of a waterfall keep interest and personal satisfaction high.

These features of the landscape must be provided with minimum disruption and environmental degradation to soils and plant life. Most important in this regard is the placement of trails on steep slopes. Gullying caused by trail erosion will soon develop on trails that climb long, steep gradients. Therefore, a happy medium must found between the trail's function of gaining elevation and the tendency of water and foot traffic to rapidly erode trails on steep grades. This happy medium can be found with a *sidehill* trail location, so that running water will

---

[3]Much of the information in this section comes from *Guidelines for the Pacific Crest National Scenic Trail*, U.S. Department of Agriculture, 1971.

# SUMMARY OF SOIL INDICATORS FOR EVALUATION OF A PROPOSED TRAIL INSTALLATION

| Conditions | Conditions Posing Slight Limitations for Trail Installations | Conditions Posing Moderate Limitations for Trail Installations | Conditions Posing Severe Limitations for Trail Installations |
|---|---|---|---|
| Soil Wetness | Depth to seasonal high water table four feet or more; well drained to moderately well drained | Depth to seasonal high water table one to four feet; excessively drained | Depth to seasonal high water table less than one foot poorly drained |
| Soil Texture | Particle mixture of sand, clay, silt; 20-50% of content gravel | High sand content; less than 50% but geater than 20% of content gravel | High clay content; no gravel |
| Soil Structure | | | Hardpans less than one foot from soil surface; peaty, muck soils |
| Soil Depth to Bedrock | Greater than three feet | 1.5 - 3 feet | Less than 1.5 feet |
| Slope | 0 - 5%* | 5 - 20% | Greater than 20% |

*Slope* is the number of feet of vertical rise per one hundred feet of horizontal distance, expressed as a percentage — that is, a 10% slope rises ten feet vertically for every hundred feet traversed horizontally.

cross the trail but not run down the treadway at high velocities that can seriously aggravate erosion. Other techniques are to break up steep climbs with short level or sidehill stretches and to provide low spots which afford natural drainage.

**Switchbacks** — To climb a long, steep grade on a mountain, sidehilling alone cannot provide the needed rise in elevation. The lateral area available for a sidehill trail is limited by terrain, so the trail must turn and start its lateral motion in the opposite direction. This turn is aptly named a *switchback*. It has been used for centuries in road and trail design.

On a well-designed trail, one switchback is not visible from another. Use is made of natural topographic features, and the length of trail segments is varied to sustain interest. Steady grades give the hiker a feeling of substantial progress in climbing.

The greatest potential for failure in switchback design is to build too many switchbacks too close together. Hikers on a trail with closely spaced switchbacks will take shortcuts, especially when descending. This in turn aggravates plant mortality and soil erosion, because the sidehill practice is nullified by direct, steep shortcuts. Watercourses and erosion will develop on such shortcuts, especially after they become trampled by large numbers of hikers.

Long stretches between switchbacks have the added advantage of requiring that fewer be built. Switchbacks, as will be seen in the next chapter, are difficult to build so that they drain properly. Keeping them few in number holds both initial construction costs and maintenance costs to manageable levels. Also, repetition is monotonous to the hiker.

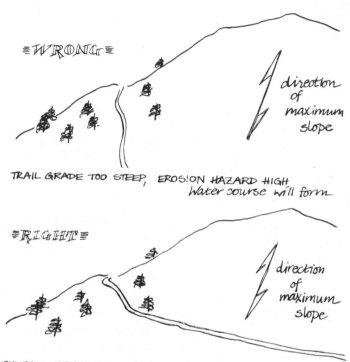

≡WRONG≡

direction
of
maximum
slope

TRAIL GRADE TOO STEEP, EROSION HAZARD HIGH
Water course will form.

≡RIGHT≡

direction
of
maximum
slope

SIDEHILL TRAIL LOCATION CONTROLS EROSION
Water crosses trail but won't flow down treadway

Another technique which can be used to control shortcutting on switchbacks is to make the switchback into a wide turn. In so doing you run the risk of having a small section of the turn running straight up the fall line. However, if the danger of shortcutting is great, as is the case in open hardwoods or above treeline where hikers can see great distances, then a wide turn running straight up the grade may be the best choice to make.

*Rock wall along fragile Franconia Ridge, N.H. channels hiker impact (facing page).*

The trail treadway on the steepest part of the turn can be hardened with soil stabilization techniques such as steps in order to keep these steep turns stable.

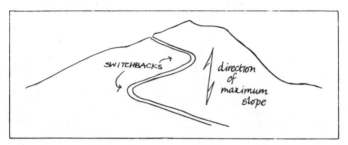

One can also make use of natural features such as rock outcrops and dense stands of vegetation as barriers to shortcutting by having them on the inside of a switchback. A viewpoint on the outer edge of a turn can sometimes prove useful in that it may attract hiker attention, drawing them to the corner rather than allowing them to notice shortcutting possibilities. Of course, switchbacks and abrupt changes in route direction must be clearly marked to prevent hikers from walking off the trail at a turn.

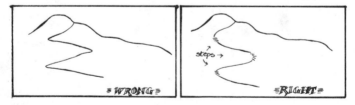

Left, *narrow switchbacks are prone to shortcutting.*
Right, *wide turns fortified with steps prevent shortcutting.*

On short, frequently used trails, such as between a water supply and a campsite or a parking lot and a view, switchbacks are best not used. They are most appropriate when designed over a large area, thus permitting adequate vegetative screening between switchback legs. Short trails do not cover enough space to permit the proper design of foolproof switchbacks.

TRAILS SHOULD TAKE ADVANTAGE OF DRAMATIC TOPOGRAPHY
Care to avoid rockfall below and excess risk above, must be balanced with the drama of the surroundings.

Rocks, cliffs, ledges, and caves provide interest in a trail location. These rigors of the landscape should not be avoided in designing a trail. Caution should be used, however, in placing trails over shale slides or talus slopes and at cliff edges. Tree scars and talus with recent fracture surfaces are a good indication that falling rock would be unreasonably dangerous under these ledges and cliffs. Trails skirting the tops of cliffs should be clearly defined and obvious to the hiker. Wet, mossy rock and ice in the spring and fall indicate that there should be reasonably cautious use of exciting cliffside trail locations. If these limiting conditions are not serious, the trail should take every advantage of dramatic topography.

Be conscious of and avoid areas with evidence of landslides, rockslides, and avalanches. (The latter, especially, should be avoided if a trail may be used in winter.) All such areas may be prone to severe soil and vegetation movement and damage and can be hazardous to hikers.

# 3

# TRAIL LAYOUT

---

TRAIL LAYOUT IS A PRACTICAL application of the information in Chapters 1 and 2. A good layout must satisfy recreational needs, as discussed in the first chapter, as well as being environmentally stable, as covered in the second chapter.

The most important work in trail installation is obviously done in the field. After the initial development of a trail proposal, the route should be checked and rechecked on location. The more time spent in this layout phase, the better the trail location will be.

Use U.S. Geological Survey (USGS) topographical maps, upon which all data can be recorded. In particularly complex layout projects, it may be helpful to make a card file that refers back to this map. In this file record all pertinent features for eventual use in the final on-the-ground layout.

Each of the cards describes the nature of a feature and whether it has a positive or negative effect on the trail; also included is any other pertinent information, such as addresses of landowners if, for instance, the particular feature is an ownership boundary on private land.

As this information file develops, each feature will become a checkpoint which must either be avoided, as in the case of a bog or a steep slope, or which will be included if its effect on the trail is positive, as would be the case with a good view. The final choice of route, then, will involve a combination of connecting positive features and circumnavigating negative ones. Overlays showing various natural, cultural, historic, and development features can be placed on a base map as an alternative — or complement — to a card file.

This layout process must also pay heed to the environmental characteristics of the landscape outlined in Chapter 2. Where possible always use a sidehill trail location, for instance, and check soil characteristics at regular intervals. Keep the gradient below 20% if possible, unless trail hardening is planned during the installation.

The layout process then becomes one of trial and error. As it proceeds, the designer will constantly be backtracking and reflagging the route until finally the location satisfies the requirements outlined in Chapters 1 and 2.

It may be helpful at this point to get professional assistance from different sources such as civil engineers, soil scientists, and foresters, who can all add their special skills to a thorough evaluation of the trail site.

A technique which may be helpful is to talk to local people, especially the older folks who are familiar with the land. These people can be extremely helpful to the trail designer, and in many cases can point out all the significant features in a particu-

lar area, as well as give a broad and personal account of its history.

Aerial photographs can reveal even to the untrained eye such features as ledges, watercourses, old logging roads potentially usable for the trail, and other detailed information on the land's characteristics. These aerial photos are available from the

USDA's Soil Conservation Service, or in the case of parks and forests from the managing agencies involved.

The trail route should be flagged with engineer's flagging tape. The color should be bright enough to stand out, and should not be the same as the prevailing colors of the fall foliage if the layout is to be done in that season. (For example, don't use yellow flagging tape in a beechwood forest in the fall.) The flagging should be placed at fairly close intervals and it should be tied securely on living trees and their branches. If the flag line has to last through a winter don't count on having a long, loose tail on a flag. It will blow off. The best technique is to tie the flag tightly around the trunk of a living tree. Use different colors to flag multiple routing possibilities so they can be differentiated.

The best time of year to do trail layout is during the spring and fall, when the leaves are off the trees and the ground is clear of ice and snow. If there is time, it is beneficial to check a trail location at several different times of the year. Checking it in winter, for instance, enables the designer to know if the trail is also appropriate for ski touring. Checking it in the spring gives an indication of drainage and wetness problems.

All of this work requires that the designer be a good outdoorsman. Skilled knowledge of map and compass, as well as demanding orienteering in a trailless area, are requirements for the job.

Trail layout is both safer and easier if the work is done by pairs. If one person stays stationary on one of the checkpoints and calls to the other, efficient layout is facilitated. Two-way radios for communication between route searchers may prove to be useful, also.

**Vegetation**

The type and density of vegetation in areas proposed for trail development have two primary functions in design:

1) An aesthetic function, enhancing the hiking experience, and
2) A management function, as a tool to assist the designer in protecting the environment.

Variety and diversity of vegetative communities along a trail route promote hiker interest and satisfaction, especially if the trail is proposed for environmental study, such as a nature trail. Likewise, continuity in species composition has its own special attraction: a prolonged stretch of dense woods can promote a hauntingly exciting feeling of anticipation and adventure. Hikers are generally interested in natural environments. In some cases, though, modified vegetation, resulting from sound timber practices, farming, or other activities, may prove to be interesting and educational, as well as valuable in providing more views and wildlife.

Obviously, there is no single criterion for making an aesthetic choice between one type of vegetative cover and another. In fact, the aesthetic quality of vegetative cover will usually be a secondary consideration. Primary emphasis in design must be placed on the characteristics of soils and topography, for these have a greater influence on trail stability in mountainous and unstable terrain.

There are several ways vegetation can be used in trail design, among them:

1) **To channel and contain hiker traffic** — Vegetation, particularly dense growth, can be used as a tool to control trail traffic. Treadway boundaries are profoundly affected by the density of trailside trees and shrubs; therefore, dense undergrowth enables greater flexibility in trail layout. For instance, switchbacks are less likely to be bypassed by overly enthusiastic hikers if dense shrubbery lines the edge of the trail.

2) **To retard trail erosion** — Roots of trailside vegetation retard soil erosion on the treadway. However, with particularly unstable soils, steep slopes, and high visitor use, this root stability is not sufficient to prevent resource damage.

3) **To protect from the weather** — Experienced hikers realize the value of tree protection, especially after having descended from the alpine zone in bad weather conditions. This aspect of vegetative cover is most important to the designer in the planning and location of campsites, where protection from the elements is a requisite of good site location.

4) **To buffer and insulate hiking activities** — An increasingly important aspect of vegetation in our crowded national parks and forests is its wonderful ability to break up lines of sight and to absorb sound. Visual and acoustical buffering of incompatible activities like off-road vehicle use guarantees that a high-quality hiking experience can, if managed properly, continue to be available on a limited land base.

A good example of the ability of vegetation to buffer sound is in snowmobile trail design. Proper buffering using vegetation, hillsides, and other features can reduce snowmobile sound levels by one-third to one-half. Vegetation is also a valuable buffer between a trail with high public use and a sensitive environment such as a pond shore.

5) **To provide building material** — As will be seen later in this book, trailside trees are a major source of building material for treadway reconstruction. The availability of trees of suitable size for treadway hardening may be a factor in whether or not a trail is routed through fragile terrain such as a bog or marsh. Native trees for hardening keep costs low and add to the natural character of a trail.

6) **To use as indications of soil characteristics** — Accurate understanding of soil conditions in an area requires direct analysis. However, cursory examination of vegetation can indicate broad soil characteristics. Tree size and age indicate soil fertility — large, young trees indicate deep, well drained soils while small, stunted trees correspondingly indicate marginal soil conditions.

The preponderance of a species can give clues to soil texture, depth, and wetness. Pine and oak are characteristic of sand soils, while fir, spruce, and hemlock indicate shallow soil depths. Swamp maple, cedar, and tamarack grow in soils that are moist and boggy for much of the year. Ground cover and understory composition can serve as a useful guide to soil characteristics.

Creative use of the vegetative character of a trail is an important part in the trail management scheme. Thoughtful design optimizes the beneficial characteristics of vegetation.

# 4

# TRAIL CLEARING

---

THE INFORMATION PRESENTED UP TO THIS point has been oriented toward building a new trail. This part of the book discusses the maintenance needs of existing trails, both in terms of basic maintenance and major rehabilitation. Most existing trail clubs and the systems they maintain face the conditions on trails that will be addressed here. Standard techniques for clearing trails are covered in this chapter.

One of the most important jobs for trail maintainers is clearing established trails. Without a regular clearing, even frequently used trails can dissolve in just four or five years into a netherworld of undergrowth.

The actual techniques for keeping trails clear will vary with the environment of the trail and with the amounts and types of visitor use the trail receives. Also, different maintainers develop and use different techniques suitable for their particular tasks and based on their individual preferences. Favorite tools and techniques can vary widely in different areas, among different organizations, and even among members of the same crew. The

point here is that you should find the best methods for you and
your organization.

## Standards

A well-cleared trail is one upon which a large hiker with a big
pack can walk erect without touching limbs, trees, or brush.
Footing is clear and the trail is easy to follow because the line of
sight, both forward and back, is open and unobstructed.
Branches of trailside shrubs, weighted down in wet weather and
snow (if it is a winter trail), will not obscure the trail.

*Before clearing East Link on Old Speck.*

*Width* — The proper width for a cleared trail varies with terrain and vegetation. A four- to six-foot clearance suffices in most situations. In thick growth a three-foot clearance may be most practical and possibly even desirable, if it provides a pleasant tunnel effect.

In high use areas and on steep slopes with thin, unstable soils, a narrow trail may be desirable to stabilize soils with the roots of trailside trees, shrubs, and grasses. It should be noted, however, that leaving trails narrow is a limited palliative; unstable soils on sloping trails under heavy user pressure will deteriorate regard-

*After clearing East Link on Old Speck.*

less of how narrow the trails are. A narrow treadway can contain trampling, though, and therefore reduce hiker impact on soils by containing it to a narrow area.

*Height* — Normally a trail is cleared to a height of eight feet, or as high as one can reach. On slopes, members of the crew can stand uphill from their work, bringing high branches more easily into reach. Where trees are large enough, a canopy should be left over the trail. This will help shade shrubs, weeds, and grasses, dampening their usually prolific growth. Correspondingly, one can enable wildflowers to grow by clearing back the canopy to let in sunlight. This can be done selectively to minimize the ''highway'' appearance of excessive clearing. In the case of a trail that is popular in winter, the maintainer may want to clear it particularly high. This will enable easier travel when snow up to three or four feet deep lies on the ground. This high clearing can be done in the summer with special tools such as a pole pruner or pole saw. However, it can be more easily accomplished with a winter trail clearing session.

## Patrolling

*Patrolling* is annual maintenance done early in the hiking season to remove winter blowdown damge from trails. In this way trails are open for use early in the hiking season, complaints are reduced, and additional work for later in the season can be assessed. AMC crews complete a 'patroller's report' after each trip. Covering trails early in the year also gives maintainers good exercise in preparation for strenuous work later in the maintenance season. Patrollers should carry an adze hoe or small mattock to clean waterbars during their travels, in addition

---

*Trailman clears trail high to avoid snags on packs and to allow for branches becoming lowered with rain and snow (facing page) .*

to their axes, bow saws, crosscuts, or chainsaws. The AMC finds the axe to be the best patrolling tool due to its light weight, ready availability, low cost, and ease of maintenance. Because its blade cannot get pinched as a saw's can, most maintainers find an axe easier to use. With proper training, it can be quite safe.

Patrolling is best done in pairs, with the workers leap-frogging from blowdown to blowdown, enabling them to patrol significant distances per day — anywhere from five to ten miles, depending on the number of blowdowns encountered and the number of waterbars to be cleaned. Pairing up also provides a measure of safety in case of unforeseen problems.

The standards already described for width and height should be applied to blowdown removal. In the most common situation a blowdown lies across the axis of a trail within six feet of the ground. This type of blowdown usually requires two cuts, one on each edge of the trail, with the center piece being removed and discarded off to the side. Some smaller blowdowns require only one cut and then the top can be thrown off the trail.

2 CUTS NEEDED TO TAKE OUT A BLOWDOWN

Other situations the patroller will meet include trees that have fallen right down the trail or trees whose tops have broken off and hang down onto the trail. Removal of these blowdowns can be time-consuming — the tree has to be cut into manageable pieces and rolled or carried off the trail. Often a "leaner" has to be cut down first to drop it into the trail and then cut into pieces for removal. Care should be exercised with leaning or hanging trees; limbs or tops can snap off and become "widow makers." Also, trees bent under tension must be cut carefully, since they may spring back. Some tree butts with roots still anchored may snap back to a vertical position when a cut is made.

With a very large blowdown, a notch or steps cut into the tree will sometimes allow passage. In certain cases it may be desirable to leave in place blowdowns that might serve as waterbars of a sort or as barriers to unwanted vehicle traffic, as long as hikers can negotiate passage over or around them. If there is no clear passage for hikers, the blowdown must be removed.

## Standardizing

*Standardizing* is one term often used to describe the technique of clearing brush next to a trail to put it into standard condition, which means that there should be adequate clearance in width and height for comfortable hiking.

Hand clippers, pruners, loppers, and bow saws are the most commonly used tools for this work. Machetes, swizzle sticks, and brush hooks are also sometimes employed. The latter often leave pointed stumps and stubs, however, and must be used carefully. Occasionally pole pruners and pole saws are needed, especially for trails used in winter and requiring high clearing. Where heavy growth exists, gasoline-powered brush cutters may be best. Be sure the operator knows how to use the equipment properly; safety should be the paramount concern. Keep all other workers well away from power equipment in use.

Low shrubs and young trees should be cut close to the ground for aesthetic reasons, to prevent tripping, and to keep stumps from sprouting. Avoid leaving potentially dangerous pointed stumps. This low growth should be removed back to the outside edge of the cleared trail. Annual growth such as ferns can be left to die later in the summer and fall unless it is particularly thick and aggravating.

Special attention should be paid to small softwoods and to the lateral branches of larger softwoods. Their needles become wet on a misty mountain day, and if brushed they get hikers quickly and surprisingly wet.

Limbs on these trees should be cut flush with the trunk or stem. Stubs are ugly and they can create bothersome and sometimes dangerous snags for packs and clothing. Branches growing toward the trail should be cut back to the next limb growing away from the trail. If trees are pruned in this way rather than being indiscriminately chopped, sucker growth will be reduced. *Sucker growth* occurs when a root system geared to provide nutrients to a tree of a certain size causes aggravated growth in the remainder of the tree when a large part is removed. By leaving growth directed away from the trail, future maintenance efforts can be reduced.

If a short treetop has to be removed, it is generally better to remove the whole tree, since removal of the terminal bud will aggravate lateral growth into the trail and leave an unsightly tree. Cutting all lateral branches on the trail side is the second best option — still better than cutting off the top of the tree only.

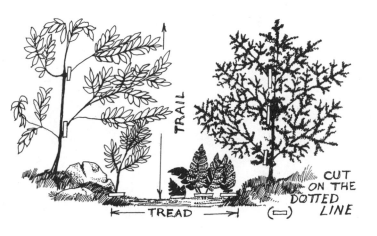

Special situations such as the following require special consideration:

1) *Alpine trails* — Judgment and temperance should be used when clearing trails near or above treeline, where the climate is severe and growth rates are very slow. Trees three to four feet tall can be sixty or seventy years old. Small trees and shrubs at treeline grow in interdependent communities called *krummholz*. Removal of one tree in a patch of krummholz can jeopardize the other trees in the patch, which join roots and branches in protection against wind and cold.

2) *Timber harvesting* — Frequently trail maintainers find that a timber operation has to cut across the trail. Clean-up and reopening of the trail involve locating and flagging the trail, then removing all slash and debris. This can require a lot of work.

## Clean-up

A good clearing job can be completely nullified if all branches and debris are not completely removed from the trail. Pick up all branches, trees, and debris and scatter them off the trail. Piles should be avoided because they are unsightly and can create a fire hazard. In some cases the trail treadway may need to be raked with a lawn rake to ensure complete clean-up and unobstructed footing. Downed trees are best dragged butt first until the top is completely off the trail. This will also serve to conceal the tree from hikers. Large limbs and small trees can be thrown clear of the trail, provided that they do not hang in the branches of shurbs and trees next to the trail or stick up butt first.

# 5

# TRAIL MARKING

---

TRAILS MUST BE MARKED in an understandable, systematic, and vandal-proof manner. This can be done with a combination of techniques, the principal ones being paint blazing, signs, and, for treeless areas, cairns. Application of the techniques will, of course, vary somewhat with each particular trail situation. For example, a short trail within a state park that is heavily used by inexperienced hikers might be extensively marked. On the other hand, it may be desirable to have sparse marking on a trail through private land in an urban area or for one in a federally designated wilderness area. Sparse marking of the former would allow it not to attract heavy or undesirable use; with the latter, light marking would be in keeping with the wild character of the area and the concept of providing challenge to hikers.

## Paint Blazing

Paint blazes are probably the most effective and commonly used technique for marking hiking trails. Paint's durability, universal availability, inexpensiveness, and ease of application probably make it the most practical method for marking most hiking trails.

In some areas plastic or metal markers of various shapes and colors are nailed to trees and posts to guide hikers. However, these markers may be removed by vandals as easily as they are put up by trail crews, while paint blazes and rock cairns cannot. They are also expensive, and color and lettering, if present, often fade after several years.

The standard blaze on the Appalachian Trail is a white 2 x 6 inch mark placed on trees and rocks. The shape of this blaze has proved to be a good, easily spotted one for trail marking. Along any trail the blazing should be consistent for its entire length. Changing the frequency of blazes can cause hikers confusion.

Likewise, there should be no gaps in the marking; the blazing should be uninterrupted. Blazes should be neat and well placed. Indiscriminate splotches can be unsightly.

**Equipment** — blazing equipment usually consists of a pint or quart of paint, a rag, a small quantity of paint thinner or brush cleaner, several paper cups, a nylon scrub pad or wire brush, one or two one-inch paintbrushes, and a 2- to 2½-inch paint scraper, all carried in a pail. Small quantities of paint in a paper cup are easier to carry, and if spilled will not result in the loss of all your paint. The rag is handy for spills or runs. Paint thinner is for cleaning the brush. The wire brush or scrub pad is used to clean rock surfaces or smooth-barked trees. The paint scraper is for smoothing spots for blazes on rough-barked trees. The pail provides a convenient way to carry all the supplies so that everything is within easy reach. Some make carrying the pail more comfortable by taping the handle or placing a short piece of old hose over it.

Water-based paints such as latex are the easiest to handle and apply, and they also dry quickly. However, latex will not last very long. Oil-based enamels, paints, or inks developed especially for boundary marking last the longest and are best to use. Recently the AMC has had good success with a brushable boundary marking ink from the American Coding and Marking Ink Company, 1220 North Avenue, Planfield, New Jersey 07062. (For other firms manufacturing such paints and inks, see a list of tool suppliers in the chapter on tools.) It is fast drying, easy to apply, and rated for five to eight years. Boundaries marked with such paints or inks are often visible for ten to fifteen years or more. Enamels or highway paints are more durable on rock surfaces.

In the installation of a new trail system or in newly marking an old trail, a standard system should be developed. Color, frequency, placement, and form should be carefully thought out before installation so that changes do not have to be made later. The best colors to use are blue, red, yellow, white, and orange. One may wish to develop a primary color for a main trail in a system and have a secondary color for side trails. This is the procedure used along the Appalachian Trail; the main route is marked in white with side trails in blue. Care should be used when the trail is located next to boundary lines. Boundaries are usually marked with paint, and if the trail blazes are of the same color confusion can result.

Blazes are placed in both fore and aft directions, perpendicular to the trail, to indicate the route of travel both ways. They should be placed on trees or rocks which "strike the eye" while traveling along the trail. A large tree is preferable to a small one and a live tree is better than a dead one. Should the dead tree blow over, the blaze will be lost. With light-colored blazes, darker trees are best for contrast, and vice versa.

A good way to determine the best tree or rock on which to place the blaze is to face down the trail ahead as one finishes painting a blaze and note quickly, at a suitable distance, a tree or rock which stands out. Walk toward it, and if it is not too far off the trail, place the next blaze on it. On a straight, wide, or well-cleared trail this may well be far ahead. One well-placed blaze is more effective than several improperly located ones.

The frequency of paint blazes will be determined by the character of the trail. On narrow woods trails with an obvious tread and trail corridor and with little opportunity for the hiker to stray off track, blazes can be widely spaced, perhaps every 100-200 feet. On the other hand, a trail without an obvious treadway through an open hardwood forest should be closely blazed — possibly every 30-50 feet. This is particularly true if the trail is used in winter. Where trails follow well-worn roads, blazes may be spaced farther apart. However, if there are many opportunities for one to turn off the road onto other roads or trails, blazing should be frequent. A good rule of thumb is that a hiker should never have to walk more than a hundred paces without being able to see a blaze either ahead of or behind him.

Do not fail to mark the trail because it is thought that no one could possibly get lost in that area. Conditions may be unexpectedly changed by new trail or road construction, lumbering, or blowdowns resulting from storms. Under such circumstances blazes at infrequent intervals may result in difficulty in following the trail. It should be borne in mind that trail marking is for the benefit of one who is unfamiliar with the trail and terrain. This consideration must be a guiding principle for trail maintainers, who may thoroughly know the terrain and route.

The usual height for blazing is 5½-6 feet — eye level for many hikers. If a trail is to be used in winter, the blazes should be slightly higher.

Immediately beyond any crossing road or trail, there must be a trail indication blaze, even though there may also be a direction sign. Because of the possibility that this blaze may disappear due to road clearing or blowdown of the tree, it is advisable to have a second, or safety, blaze nearby, perhaps twenty to fifty feet from the crossing. This serves as insurance if the primary marking of the crossing is obliterated.

At important changes in the route, such as turns into a less well defined trail or road, there should be two disconnected blazes of the prescribed size, one two inches above the other. This double blaze serves as a warning to the hiker: "Stop . . . Look!" The direction of the turn is not indicated with this method. Some trail maintainers are experimenting with offset double blazes to indicate direction, the top blaze being slightly offset in the direction of the turn.

To ensure adequate and proper spacing, it is desirable when possible for blazing to be treated as a separate job for each direction — that is, blazes should be painted in one direction at a time. Where possible avoid placing blazes on both sides of the same tree, since the loss of one tree will result in a twofold loss in marking.

Paint should not be applied until the surface of a tree or rock has been prepared. On rock, a wire brush or nylon scrub pad works well to scrape off dirt and lichen. On softwoods with smooth, thin bark and on hardwoods with smooth bark, the same tools also work well. On trees with rough bark, such as hemlock or oak, a paint scraper can be used to scrape a flat, fairly smooth surface the size of the paint blaze. Do not cut through the bark on any tree, as it will damage the tree and resin will ooze out, discoloring the blaze. Also, do not blaze during rainy or damp weather, since paint will run and will probably not adhere to surfaces.

*The tree surface should be prepared for painting using a hardwood floor scraper.*

From time to time it becomes necessary to obliterate paint blazes. The reason for this may be extensive relocation of a section of trail, a slight change due to some recent obstruction such as a beaver flowage, recent growth which has obstructed

*After the surface has been prepared, the paint can easily be applied.*

the view of a blaze, or a need to standardize the marking of a trail section which has been improperly marked. When renewing blazes, portions of old blazes which have been widened by tree growth need to be obliterated. To eliminate all or a portion of a blaze, use a brown, gray, or custom-mixed paint matched to the surface being covered. An enamel paint, brushable or in a spray can, is best.

When a trail is relocated, all blazes on the abandoned section should be obliterated. It is not sufficient to simply eliminate those at each end, since persons straying onto the old route may see the blazes in between, assume they are on the trail, and be greatly misled, possibly with unfortunate results. (There have been such cases, resulting in criticism of the maintaining group involved.)

## Signs

Signs are an essential component of any trail. Most signs indicate the trail name, direction, highlights, facilities, and distances. Some also have a symbol or abbreviation of the maintaining organization(s). In addition to trail signs, some

trails have special markers made of plastic or metal that refer to a special designation or point out that the trail is part of a specific trail system. These markers are usually placed at trailheads and sometimes are hung at intervals along the trail as well. Several different types of signs are discussed in this section, along with information on their fabrication, installation, and maintenance.

**Wooden Routed Signs** — The most common trail signs are made of wood, with the lettering cut into the sign with a router. Because the lettering is actually cut into the wood, the sign will be legible even after all paint or stain has worn off through weathering.

**Fabrication of Wooden Routed Signs** — Routing wooden signs is a time-consuming process that requires skill and patience. However, any person with an artistic bent and the proper equipment can make professional looking signs using this method. Several tricks can also be used to make the job easier and faster. (Commericial routers with templates are also available but are very expensive.)

**Type of Wood** — The choice of wood to be used should take into account characteristics such as workability, durability, and strength, as well as availability and cost. The best woods are clear heart redwood, bass wood, Ponderosa yellow pine, white pine, or western fir. In the southeastern United States cyprus and locust are often used. Get good-quality stock, straight and free of knots.

**Size of Sign Board** — Boards one inch thick are appropriate for most routed wooden signs. At trailheads, where large descriptive signs are needed, two-inch stock may be best. The length and width of the sign varies with the length of the message and with the sign's importance. Trailhead signs may be as large as two by three feet, whereas directional arrows can be as small as three by eight inches. Because hikers stand directly in front of a trail sign, it is not necessary to make it large, except for the sign at the roadside. Large signs can be made from several boards joined with dowel joints, threaded rods, or something similar.

SOME DIFFERENT JOINTS FOR 2" SIGN STOCK

DOVETAIL          LAP SPLINE          DOWEL PINNED
   SPLINE        screws countersunk
        ALL CONTACTING SURFACES GLUED

**Size of Lettering** — Most signs will not need lettering larger than 1½ inches in height. This large lettering can be used for the name of a trail so it will stand out. The text of a sign is usually then done with lettering ½ or ¾ inch in height.

**Stencils** — Stencils should be used when laying out the text of a sign. Plastic or metal stencils can be obtained from a sign manufacturer, but they are fairly expensive. It may be better to simply visit the local stationery or art supply store. Many of them sell inexpensive paper stencils for tracing letters of different sizes. Some maintainers, rather than lay out signs from scratch time and time again, particularly large signs, lay out the text on high-quality drafting paper. This can be placed over the sign board with carbon paper in between and the text lightly traced, producing a carbon outline on the sign board. The text can then be filed away for future use. Such reusable texts can also save time when making multiples of one sign or where certain words or lines of text are repeated.

**Routing** — Before routing text laid out on a sign, practice on scrap wood. Considerable skill is needed to get professional results. Practice will make perfect.

A sharp bit is essential to good lettering. A dull bit will leave "feathers" that will have to be sanded out or that will be ugly if painted. A dull bit will also burn the wood. A carbide-tipped bit, V-shaped or U-shaped, should be used. Carbide steel is extremely hard and will last a long time if used properly. If a V-shaped bit is used, it can be raised or lowered when routing to create letters of different width and depth. A U-shaped bit can also be used in this manner to some extent. When routing large letters, it is sometimes best to do it initially with a V-shaped bit, followed by a U-shaped. This facilitates the routing. As the U-shaped bit has more surface area, it tends to work harder and may overheat. Taking out some of the wood with a V-shaped bit makes it easier for the U-shaped bit to make its pass. If you make a mistake you can often repair it with a little plastic wood. If a router bit is used on plywood it may be irreparably damaged because of the hard glue used to join the layers of plywood.

When using the router always wear safety goggles to protect the eyes from wood shavings or defective bits.

**Painting and Staining** — Generally two colors are used on a sign, one for the background and one for the lettering. Some simply stain the entire sign; others first stain and then paint the lettering with enamel. When using stains, some coat the sign with a polyurethane or varnish for further protection. The entire sign can also be painted with the background in one color and the lettering painted over this first coat in another. A good-quality enamel should be used. Latex does not last very long. Great patience should be used when painting the letters. This should be done with a small brush. Some also use a small nail or syringe to fill the routed letter with paint. One trick the AMC sign man uses to facilitate letter painting is to stencil the sign text on the board, cover the face of the sign with contact paper, and then route through it. He then quickly brushes paint into the lettering and pulls off the contact paper. Generally very little touch up is needed. The contact paper, however, does tend to dull the router bit more quickly.

**Hanging the Sign** — Since signs, particularly attractive ones, may be prone to theft and vandalism, secure hanging techniques should be employed. A technique the AMC has used successfully is to mount the sign on a backboard cut from two-inch stock. The backboard is nailed or lag-bolted to a tree or post, and the sign is then bolted to the backboard. Using sign backing also protects the sign from splitting due to tree growth. And it provides a more secure mounting. Small signs can be held to the backboard with two bolts. They should be slightly offset so as not to split the sign along the grain. Larger signs need four bolts. All bolts, washers, and nails should be galvanized or at least zinc plated. Standard ones will rust, leaving an unsightly stain on the sign.

Signs that are often stolen can be mounted using special nuts and bolts, such as Vandlgard or Tufnut brands (Vandlgard, Voi-Shan, 8463 Higuera Street, Box 512, Culver City, California 90230, and Tufnut Works, 236 Montezuma Sreet, Santa

Fe, New Mexico 87501). Bolts can also be countersunk and the tops covered with wooden plugs or wood putty. Numerous techniques have been employed by maintainers to reduce theft. One is to bolt the sign with a small piece of chain looped around the tree. It may be possible to work the sign loose, but the chain still attaches it to the tree. Grease has been applied to the back of signs, and some have even been wrapped in barbed wire. Others have been placed high out of reach, and some have been painted on ledge or large rocks.

The most attractive and effective method of hanging signs is probably to use a signpost. Trees are not always available or in the right location in the field. Also, posts eliminate damage to trees. A six- to ten-inch diameter post, buried to a depth of three feet, is usually best. Use a softwood tree such as a cedar, locust, or hemlock, since they will last the longest. Posts used at accessible trailheads might be pressure treated or at least treated on site before installation. Posts should also be peeled.

The upper end of the post should be beveled with an axe. To prevent turning or removal of the post, one or two threaded rods, pieces of rebar, or a large spike can be placed into or through the bottom of the post before it is buried. Another method is to nail one or two pieces of wood onto the bottom of the post. Posts placed in stone cairns above treeline should definitely be installed in this manner. The sign should be attached to the post on a flattened surface. It can be nailed or bolted.

**Master Sign List** — A master sign list for the trail system should be developed by the maintainer. This list documents the location of all signs, the text of each, and the size of each sign board. With a system such as this, maintenance, repairs, and replacement are facilitated. All AMC signs are numbered and keyed to the master list. The number is painted on the back of the sign and routed into the backboard for easy viewing.

**Temporary Signs** — If permanent signs are not ready when a trail is to be opened or if an important sign is stolen, a temporary sign should be erected in its place. Heavy poster-board and permanent, waterproof ink, such as that from a magic marker, can be used to make good temporary signs. The finished product can be encased in contact paper to waterproof the sign. Such a sign stapled and glued to plywood and hung on a tree should easily last one to two years. It should be checked for fading and damage from squirrels and birds if it must serve longer than that. A dark-colored ink should be used. Red and light colors tend to fade quickly.

**Other Signs** — Some maintainers make signs by simply using a stencil and painting outlined letters on a board. This is a very tedious and time-consuming task, however, and should the paint or painted letters come off the text will be illegible. We have seen a few signs which were made from plate steel, with letters made with a bead of brazing or stenciled and cut out with a torch. Both techniques are costly, and such signs are generally not very aesthetic in a backwoods setting. For vandal-prone areas they may be desirable, however. Some also use wooden or concrete post signs where the text is routed or cast into the post itself. Since these can be securely buried and tend to be very long and heavy, theft is less of a problem.

## Cairns and Posts

Marking trails in treeless areas requires the construction of conspicuous rock piles known as *cairns*. In the absence of rock, posts have been used. Cairns make attractive and natural trail markers and are often effective year-round because of their visibility even under the snow and ice conditions of winter. Well-placed and well-built cairns also help protect the fragile soils of alpine areas by keeping people on a single trail. Cairns are especially important when the weary traveler must find the way in the poor visibility of an alpine storm.

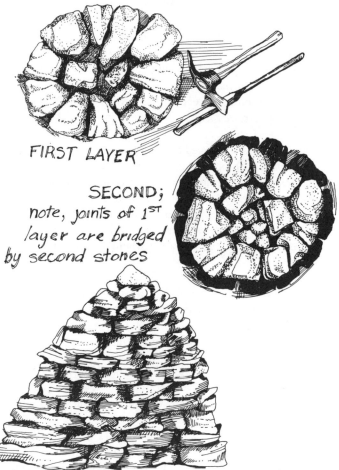

FIRST LAYER

SECOND;
note, joints of 1ˢᵀ
layer are bridged
by second stones

A WELL MADE CAIRN; rocks lean
toward center, and joints are
broken.

Cairns should be between fifty and a hundred feet apart. They should be placed along trails that have been laid out in a fairly direct fashion. People will shortcut sharp turns; therefore, it is best to keep the trail curving with the land in gentle undulations. Such trails take the easiest route and, therefore, represent the most likely choice of travel for the average hiker, who is typically committed to economizing on the effort it takes to traverse any terrain.

Cairns should be placed at conspicuous locations: a knoll is obviously a better location than a hollow. If a ledge or mound is available, then the cairn has greater visibility if placed on it. Occasionally light-colored rocks can be found and used for the top of the cairn, making it more visible. Some paint the upper rock. Paint blazes are also used in conjunction with cairns to mark the route, especially in areas where rock for cairn building is scarce.

**Construction of Cairns** — Cairns should be built to the height of three to five feet. They should be fairly squat, almost as wide at the base as they are high. Cairns constructed in this manner effectively resist weather and tampering by hikers.

Occasionally cairns have to be smaller when rock for construction is unavailable. Care should be used to avoid damage in quarrying rock in areas with fragile soils and vegetation. In some cases it is better to depend upon wooden posts and paint blazes. Large flat rocks should be used in cairns, especially for the base layer. Each layer should slope towards the center of the cairn. If this method is used for each succeeding tier, gravity will tend to stabilize the cairn's construction in much the same way a stone arch is strengthened by a keystone. Each stone placed on a cairn should have at least three points of contact. Then each rock placed will be stable and will not wiggle.

Wedging small stones into cracks between large rocks to stabilize them is not a good practice. These wedges may work loose, resulting in loose rocks in the cairn. Each stone should be stabilized with its neighbor stones. In this way a strong cairn will result.

## Marking Systems

There is a growing need for development of a widely recognized marking system for hiking trails. Different trail groups in different states are grappling with various experimental techniques: plastic diamonds, metal arrows, and different quality paints are all being evaluated.

*Examples of various trail markers.*

This process is a good one and should be accelerated. Trail constituents need a system which will be easily recognized and accepted by all users of trail lands, including landowners, off-road vehicle users, and hikers. With a standard system trails may become more widely accepted as a facility that is an essential part of the local community.

# 6

# GUIDELINES FOR TRAIL RECONSTRUCTION

---

ALL LAND AREAS HAVE AN INHERENT and variable
ability to sustain recreational use without suffering damage to
soils, vegetation, and water. This ability can be relatively low,
especially in mountain parks and forests with steep slopes and
abundant water runoff. To increase the land's ability to withstand hiking use without resource damage, trail construction
techniques need to be introduced.

The intensity, and consequently the expense, of construction
of a satisfying and undamaged trail environment is controlled
basically by two factors. The first is the volume of use an area
receives. As use increases there is more wear and tear on a trail,
and therefore the need for increased trail stabilization work is
present if soils and plant life are to be maintained in a healthy
condition. The second factor governing construction is the
character of the land itself. Areas that are wet, located on steep
slopes, characterized by poor soils, or which support fragile
vegetation such as that present in the alpine zone require particularly careful — and sometimes costly — construction. There
are construction techniques which allow a certain degree of use

in such areas, but the associated costs of labor and materials will be high and an inevitable loss of natural qualities will result. Trails in these more sensitive areas should be avoided if possible — or at least minimized.

## When to Relocate

Gullies or wide muddy areas on trails can be tackled in one of two ways: they can be circumnavigated with a relocated section of trail or they can be hardened with techniques described later. When deliberating on this choice, two questions should be answered.

1) *Will the new section of trail have the same environmental conditions and the same design as the damaged section being replaced?*

Often the answer to this question is "yes," which means that the same steep slope or boggy soils have to be traversed by the relocated section of the trail. If this is the case, then more often than not it is best to stick to the old location rather than opening up a new one that will deteriorate in the same fashion. If, however, the same terrain is crossed but in a less direct fashion — i.e., if there is a design change whereby the trail crosses the slope rather than climbs directly up it — then the relocation is probably worth considering. The same environmental conditions may predominate, but the trail design in this case is more topographically sound.

2) *Will the old section of the trail be too difficult to close and rehabilitate?*

If the section of trail being replaced is the most obvious location in a given landscape — for example, on a pond shore or on a pronounced ridge — then hikers naturally tend to assume its existence and will use the trail even after a relocation is installed and the section in question has been closed. In these cases, again, it is best to stick to the old location. Sometimes in situations like this, a relocation can actually hasten environmental degradation by becoming confused with the old location so that hikers begin using both routes interchangeably. When this happens there can be many problems with both locations, as well as any unplanned crossover trails that may develop because of hikers' confusion.

Generally relocations should only be used when there can be a substantial improvement in the environmental conditions on the new section. This assumes that the relocation will replace a substantial piece of trail. Short relocations around a wet area may be appropriate, but the best long-term solution is usually to either close and replace a long trail section or to reconstruct it. More often than not the hardening alternative is the best one; it will be addressed in the next two chapters.

## Building Materials for Reconstruction

The techniques described here require that the trail maintainer find native materials in the vicinity of the trail and move them to the treadway for use in its reconstruction. This laborious process should be undertaken carefully to minimize damage to the trail environment and to maximize the quality of reconstruction.

The materials, usually wood or rock, are either cut or dug from sites near the trail but preferably out of sight from it. This is a primary criterion in choosing reconstruction materials — that they be unnoticed and subtle in terms of what the trail user senses as he traverses a trail's length.

**Wood Materials** — Usually a stand of trees appropriate in size and length can be found uphill and out of sight of the trail. After the trees are cut down they should be limbed, peeled, and cut to appropriate length on site so that bark, wood chips, and other waste products are not left on the trail itself. Once prepared they can be hand carried to the trail. A peeled log can be slippery, however, so some prepare the log at the trail and remove the debris afterward.

**Rock Materials** — Rock debris should also be removed out of sight of the trail. Dead brush and other forest litter should be placed in any hole left by removal of rock near the trail. So as not to leave a visible scar, do not cut bedrock or ledge within sight of a trail.

**Soil for Fill** — Occasionally a soil pit needs to be dug to provide soil for fill work along the trail. Though such pits can be near the trail, they should be out of direct view, and after being used they should be filled with debris and hidden.

**Service Trails** — In major construction projects it is best to gather building materials in several locations and then transport

them to the trail using limited access routes. In this manner damage to surrounding areas is reduced by being contained to feeder trails which, after construction, can be closed, covered with debris, and rehabilitated.

## Rock Work

Sometimes the trail maintainer is confronted with an obvious solution to a classic trail problem, but because of sparse tree growth or lack of rock, adequate building materials cannot be secured. There are, however, specialized techniques which, with the proper equipment, can be used to develop rock building materials from scanty resources.

Bedrock or large boulders can be split into manageable pieces using a gas-powered jackhammer. Two kinds are commercially available, and both are designed to be used in remote locations. (See pages 210-211 and the tool listing in Chapter 12.). The unit, plus gasoline and accessories, can be packed into remote locations to split rock for crews. With practice, patience, and a good supply of suitable rock, a two-man team can provide material for a building crew.

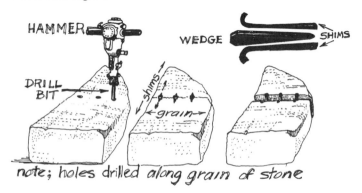

note; holes drilled along grain of stone

Jackhammers are used to drill holes in rock along its grain. (Rock, like wood, has grain — i.e., an axis plane along which there is a natural weakness.) Shims are placed along the sides of each hole in the rock being split, and wedges are placed between the shims. These are alternately driven with a small sledgehammer until the rock splits.

When installing rock that has been split from a larger rock with a jackhammer, it is beneficial, if possible, to put the split side down and out of sight. The drill holes are unsightly and can detract from the appearance of the trail.

The jackhammer can also be used to anchor steel bars or pipes for steps, signposts, railings, or hand and foot loops of reinforcing rod on steep ledges. Reinforcing rod, coordinated in size with drill bit diameters, can be anchored into rock using a special hydraulic cement that expands when it dries, securing the steel in the ledge. Discretion should be used in these situations, because trails that are so steep they require artificial aids such as railings and hand and foot loops may not be well suited for popular foot trails.

**Felling a Tree**

Tree cutting is a skill that can be improved even after years of experience. The inexperienced cutter should learn on small-diameter trees; he will learn fastest if he has instruction from someone with experience. With practice the novice can graduate to larger-diameter trees and to more complex cuts that require much pre-planning and forethought.

Several factors must be considered in order to fell a tree in the direction desired:

1) *The direction and strength of the wind* — It is easiest to fell a tree downwind or at right angles to a mild wind. It is hardest to fell a tree into a strong wind.

*Woodsman studies tree carefully before executing the backcut that will complete felling operation.*

2) *The lean of the tree* — It is easiest to fell a tree in the direction it is leaning or at right angles to the lean. With big trees, particularly hardwoods, it can be difficult to determine the lean. The cutter has to study the tree carefully and try to determine the relative weights of the major limbs.

3) *Other trees in the area* — Great care should be used when felling to ensure that a tree does not get hung up in a neighboring tree halfway down. A hung-up tree can be very troublesome and, when the cutter tries to get it down, potentially very dangerous. The safest way to get a hung-up tree down is to drag the butt back from the direction of the fall. In choosing the direction for felling, space will ideally be available so that the tree will fall all the way to the ground.

**Safety Procedures** — There are several rules of safe felling which should always be followed:

1) The tree should be carefully studied to determine if it has any dead limbs that could break off during the cutting. In logging terminology these are called ''widow makers,'' and for obvious reasons trees with these limbs should also be avoided.

2) The area around the base of the tree should be thoroughly cleared so that the cutter will not be restricted, confined, or have his concentration disturbed during the cut.

3) An exit route away from the direction of the fall should be cleared, and its use should be rehearsed several times so that in the event that something unpredictable happens the cutter can move quickly out of the danger area. This escape route will also be used after the tree starts its

fall. If the fall line of the tree is uncertain, then more than one escape route should be prepared. Once the tree starts to fall, the cutter should get out of the vicinity of the cut because of the danger of "kickback" from the butt of the tree.

TRIM OUT THE PUCKERBRUSH

**The Cut** — The first cut in a tree to be felled is the *scarf*, which is on the side of the trunk in the direction of the planned fall line. The scarf depth should be one-fifth to one-half the diameter of the trunk. If no heart rot is evident, a deeper scarf will better guarantee that the tree falls in a predictable manner.

Proper preparation of the scarf ensures a predictable fall line. The scarf should be a perfect "V" shape, with no wood chips left at the point of the "V." Any wood chips left will tend to wedge the tree off the planned fall line. The fall line will be exactly at right angles to the back of the scarf, all other factors being equal.

After preparation of the scarf, the *backcut* is begun. At this time it is wise to check to make sure no fellow workers are in the vicinity of the fall line. Those in the area should be aware of the progress of the cut. Also, it is a good practice to check escape routes one final time before proceeding.

The backcut should be slightly higher than the scarf. In this way the tree will fall in the direction of the scarf.

As the backcut is made a "hinge" will be formed from the remaining wood between the scarf and the backcut. As the cutter finishes the back cut he should watch for the first, almost imperceptible movement of the tree. If it is in the desired direction he can proceed. Minor adjustments in the direction of fall can be made by cutting the side of the hinge opposite the direction of fall desired. For example, if the tree begins to twist to the right, the cutter would deepen the back cut in the left side.

As soon as the fall begins, the cutter should immediately leave the scene along one of the pre-planned escape routes. Tree butts frequently kick back or sideways.

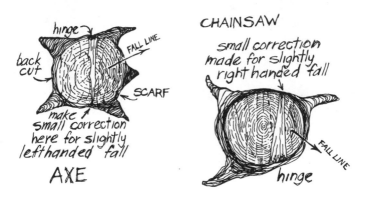

If a tree gets hung up in another, becoming a "leaner," sometimes a few bounces, pushes, or kicks to the butt of the cut will knock it loose. A crowbar, cant hook, or peavy can be used to roll or twist a tree butt to free the top. A winch or rope can also be used. Extreme care should be exercised in any such activity. Removal of the tree holding the cut tree should be a last resort; if it must be done, do it very carefully, since it will be under tension and the leaner will be hanging in it above the cutter.

# 7

# EROSION CONTROL

---

THE MOST DIFFICULT TASK IN MAINTAINING trails over steep, mountainous terrain is establishing a stable soil situation on popular routes. In the chapter on soils and topography the problem was addressed in terms of the initial layout of the trail. The merits of relocation in areas that exhibit poor trail design and layout have also been discussed. Now we will look at the techniques that are needed to "reconstruct" and maintain a healthy soil situation on existing trails. Many techniques outlined here and in subsequent chapters are the workaday techniques used by the AMC trail crew.

When constructing or reconstructing a trail, one should attempt to minimize the visual impact of trail work and to avoid undue infringement on the natural qualities of the trail. Overconstruction or excessively regular and obviously man-made construction can degrade the trail environment as much as the erosion such building was designed to prevent.

*Waterbars* and *steps* are the two main weapons the trail maintainer has in his erosion control arsenal. Waterbars can be considered a dynamic form of erosion control and steps a static form. The maintainer should keep in mind that these are not only erosion control techniques, but also erosion preventative techniques; in other words, trails should be waterbarred as a preventative measure, even if erosion is not yet evident.

Waterbars, set at an angle across the trail, direct the water off the trail. Steps, set perpendicular to the trail, serve to slow the water down and to retain soil, reducing the steepness of the slope and creating little terraces. The two techniques complement each other, and should be used jointly.

Tools generally needed for building waterbars and steps include a single bit axe, pick mattock, and small bow saw. Waterbars should always be peeled to inhibit rot and prevent insect damage; therefore, a peeler or bark spud, which will greatly facilitate peeling, should also be available. If using rock, a twelve- to twenty-pound crowbar and a shovel are needed in addition to a pick mattock. An old axe or pruner for cutting roots expedites digging.

## Wood Waterbars

Any rot-resistant type of wood can be used for a waterbar. Usually the maintainer has to use what is readily available. Spruce and fir are the usual choices in the northeast, since they can be cut and peeled easily and are relatively lightweight and easily carried. Hardwood can also be good, but in the large dimensions required for good waterbars they are very difficult to hand carry. Conifers such as hemlock, fir, spruce, and cedar also tend to be a good deal more rot-resistant than common hardwoods such as beech or birch.

The diameter of a waterbar should be at least six to eight inches at the log's small end. The length depends on the width of the trail, which in some cases can be more than ten feet. It should extend past the outside edge of the treadway on both sides. Neither water nor people should be able to go around either end of the bar; otherwise, channeling and soil compaction will misdirect water and nullify the waterbar's purpose. Large logs can sometimes be carried to the trail on the shoulders of two or more workers. Where woods are open, timber carriers may also be used.

A TOO-SHORT BAR WOULD ALLOW THE WATER TO TAKE THIS PATH

BE SURE THE WATERBAR FULLY REMOVES THE WATER SO THAT IT CANNOT FIND ITS WAY BACK ONTO THE TRAIL

Ideally, water should be channeled from the trail without its flow being significantly impeded, thereby preventing it from dropping its load of sediment and clogging the bar. For this reason, natural turns in the trail can be excellent waterbar locations because the bar in this situation will be self-cleaning, an important factor in considering locations.

Waterbars may tend to misdirect hikers, especially on corners. Barricading with dead brush or rock will properly direct hikers who might be led astray by drainage ditches. Be careful not to plug up the ditches.

THE TRAIL TAKES THE TURN

AND THE WATER GOES STRAIGHT

Once the water is well off the trail, placement of log and rock impediments should be considered to slow the water down and remove its energy without damaging trailside soils. This is especially important if water falls or drops steeply off the trail. Rocks or scree, like an object placed at the base of a gutter on a house, should be used in this situation; otherwise, erosion undermining the lower side of the trail might be a problem. In the alpine zone, where plants are small and easily disturbed, this can be a particularly vexing situation.

**Placement** — The first and most important step in the construction of a waterbar is deciding where it should be placed. Only by thoroughly planning placement, angle, and length will the maintainer build an effective waterbar.

On a steep slope where erosion is occurring, water must be removed at the top of the slope before damage can occur. Try to

*Rocks dissipate force of runoff.*

locate where the water comes onto the trail, and look for ways to remove it quickly. Look for evidence of seeps or springs. Leaf litter and debris deposits showing water movement after spring snow melt or rain storms can often be found. When a small stream or some other form of runoff enters a trail, walk up the watercourse before waterbarring to see if it can be channeled away before it reaches the trail. Sometimes jams of debris will develop, causing water that was never affecting the trail before to come onto it. Clearing the debris will often return the water to its original channel. Where numberous small runoffs cross a trail, it may be possible through ditching to channel the water into one main flow, thus avoiding excessive construction. At stream crossings, where there is a possibility of the flow jumping the channel and going down the trail, a waterbar might be necessary to stabilize and reinforce the lower stream bank. Usually a combination of steps and waterbars is used, though if soils are quite stable and slopes are not steep then waterbars alone may be all that is necessary.

Spacing depends on the steepness of slope and the availability of places to divert the water off the trail. In a gully or on a poorly laid-out section of trail, placement choices are usually few in number. On grades of 20% or more, every opportunity to remove water should be taken.

Creative placement of bars and steps in a complementary sequence prevents the bars from clogging with loose soil held in check by steps. Steps are in turn protected by waterbars that remove water from the trail and therefore keep the steps from washing out.

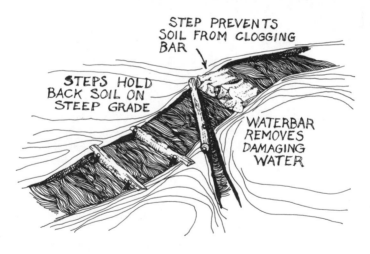

In steep-sided gullies where removal of water is difficult, steps may predominate. However, every possible exit for water should have a waterbar, even if it requires digging through the walls of the gully.

**Installation** — Once a site is chosen, the first step is to dig a trench that will hold the waterbar. In order to divert the water efficiently, the waterbar and its trench must be at an angle, generally 30 to 40 degrees to the treadway. Too shallow an angle will result in the water slowing down and dropping soil that will eventually clog it. Too sharp an angle, perhaps in excess of 70 degrees, may accelerate runoff, undermining the waterbar and increasing erosion damage.

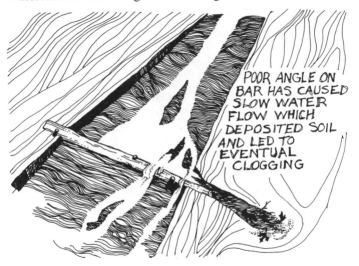

POOR ANGLE ON BAR HAS CAUSED SLOW WATER FLOW WHICH DEPOSITED SOIL AND LED TO EVENTUAL CLOGGING

The depth of the trench should be about the same as the diameter of the waterbar, enabling it to be almost flush with the trail on its downhill side once in place. Too shallow a trench may leave the waterbar sticking up too high and increase the danger of water washing out underneath the log.

The ditch should be at least as long as the log, and in most cases greater. On the lower end, to ensure that the water is directed well off the trail, the trench is usually extended one to three feet beyond the end of the log, unless natural topography adequately channels water away from the trail.

After the trench is dug and the log fitted into it, the waterbar can be staked securely in place. Hardwood or softwood saplings, two to three inchs in diameter, can be cut into two- to three-foot lengths using a bow saw. The lower ends are usually sharpened with an axe. If the upper ends are shaved slightly all around with an axe, the stakes are often less prone to split when being pounded.

CROSS -
SECTION
OF SOIL AROUND
WATERBAR

Three to five stakes can be used, one at the lower end of the waterbar and one or two on each side of it. Stakes on the uphill side of the bar should be notched into the log for added security and to minimize drag when water passes. When placing stakes, drive them in at an angle to form an inverted "V" over the log. This way the stakes fit tightly against the bar and actually hold the log down. Stakes should not stick up above the log, but should be driven or cut flush with the top of the waterbar. Use a sledgehammer or an old single bit axe for pounding. Do not use a good axe, since pounding can distort the axe eye.

## STAKES

good                    bad

A drawback with stakes is that after some wear and soil settling they may begin to stick up and form potentially hazardous projections to catch on pant cuffs and boots of hikers. Stakes may also get kicked out if hit repeatedly by hiker traffic. Keep them cut flush with the top of the log and placed near each end of it, out of the main flow of traffic. Or, a better solution might be to fit the bar into the terrain in a precise manner, minimizing the need for stakes.

Large rocks can also be placed on each end of a waterbar. This is preferable to stakes, in that rocks are more aesthetic and permanent. Sometimes they are the only choice if soils are rocky or hard, making stake driving impossible. Rocks can also serve as barriers to prevent hikers from going around one end or the other. Sometimes, with good planning and skillful use of tools, one can wedge a waterbar between existing boulders in the trail.

USE ROCKS TO ANCHOR A WATERBAR WHEN THE SOIL IS TOO THIN TO TAKE A STAKE

**Drainage Ditch** — A drainage ditch may be used to collect water above the bar in areas where the soil is saturated by heavy seepage or where many little springs exist. If a trail is ditched on its uphill side, water traveling laterally through the soil will be caught in the ditch before it hits the tread of the trail. Then, after traversing the length of the ditch, it will be carried off by the waterbar.

DRAINAGE
DITCH and BAR

In evaluating a trail section's drainage, use a ditch wherever necessary to develop permanent drainage patterns that will leave the trail treadway hard and dry. With practice, trail workers develop a sense of what is required to drain and harden wet soils on trails on mountain slopes. On steep slopes any collection ditches should be drained by frequent waterbars to avoid excessive buildups of water, which may exacerbate erosion. Extremely large and unsightly ditches should be avoided for aesthetic reasons.

**Drainage of a Switchback** — If a switchback needs to be drained, one method is to direct water on the upper leg of the switchback to its upper side. Then the water, with the use of a ditch, can be properly and completely drained at the apex of the switchback, as illustrated below.

In some cases it may be necessary to drain water off the low side of the upper switchback. If this situation is encountered, a second waterbar on the lower leg of the switchback may be necessary to remove water completely, as shown in the second drawing.

**Final Steps of Installation** — Once the waterbar is secure, pack soil up against its downhill side. This should be a good-sized mound, eight to twelve inches wide and slightly higher

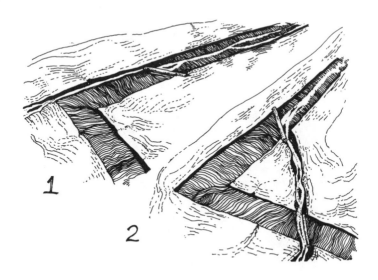

than the top of the waterbar. With traffic it will pack and wear down flush. Some bury the entire log in a mound. On the uphill side pack some soil underneath the log to prevent water from undercutting it.

The ditch above the waterbar should be backsloped. A steep-sided ditch will only collapse with hiker traffic, and water flow and debris will clog the waterbar. The drainage ditch off the end of the waterbar should be broad (6-8 inches or more), free of roots, and the sides should be sloped. A narrow ditch or one with roots in it will clog easily; steep sides are apt to collapse. A well-placed and properly secured bar can be almost mainte-nance-free. During the life of a good bar it will channel water and deposit sediments in such a way as to cause beneficial drainage patterns even after the wood of the waterbar has rotted and begun to deteriorate.

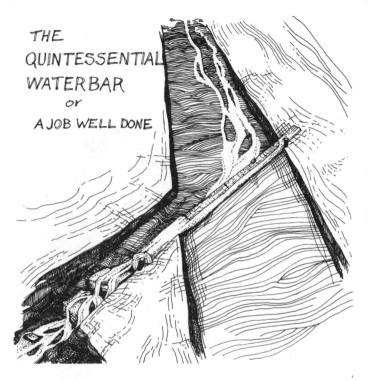

THE
QUINTESSENTIAL
WATERBAR
or
A JOB WELL DONE

An important final step is to top a portion of the waterbar with
an axe, making it rough-surfaced for good footing. This is
especially true for logs that have not been peeled, since the log
will be very slippery once the bark rots.

**Waterbar Maintenance** — Waterbars should be cleaned
out annually in order to keep them working at maximum effectiveness. Deposited soil, leaf litter, and organic matter will clog
waterbars, especially those which are not self-maintaining. Debris should be dug out on the upper side, with sediments being
spread over the trail below the bar to backfill it. Any ditch that

has filled in should be cleaned at the same time, using the debris for backfill. Don't throw it off the trail and waste it. An adze hoe or hazel hoe works well. Sometimes soils can be too compacted to be easily dug out with a shovel.

*Cleaning waterbar — soil from ditch is used to reinforce mound.*

## Rock Waterbars

These are not too commonly used, since suitable rock is generally not available. The principles of construction are basically the same as for a log waterbar.

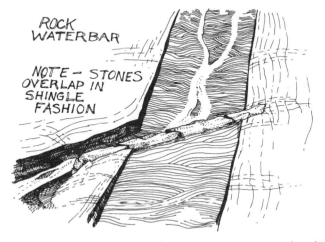

Generally, flat and narrow rock is set into a narrow but deep trench. If the rocks are butted end to end tightly or overlapped in shingle fashion, water will not go between them. Placed solidly and properly, rock waterbars can provide a longer lasting and more aesthetic alternative to peeled log waterbars. They are, for obvious reasons, more appropriate above treeline.

**Drainage Dips** — Drainage dips, often used on logging roads, are another water removal technique. Briefly, this technique involves digging a trench across the trail at an angle and making a fairly substantial mound (one to two feet high and equally thick) on the downhill side with the soil. Only if soils are quite stable is this effective; the mound can quickly break down from the forces of water and hiking traffic. Dips should be dug at a sharp angle (45-50 degrees) to reduce the force of the flowing water and subsequent erosion against the mound. For added strength in the construction of drainage dips, logs or rocks can be laid under the mound as a foundation for the soil. Dips require more maintenance than waterbars. In addition to keeping the ditch clear, the mound should be built up periodically with more soil.

DRAINAGE DIP — CROSS SECTION

## Steps

Though probably less important in reconstruction than waterbars, steps grow in importance as trail slopes steepen. If a trail has moderate grades, steps are needed infrequently and are usually confined to locations just above waterbars, where they help prevent clogging. However, on steep ascents they are critical to soil retention and stabilization. The basic purpose of steps is to provide a stable vertical rise on the trail while permitting lower average grades between steps. This slows water and retains soil.

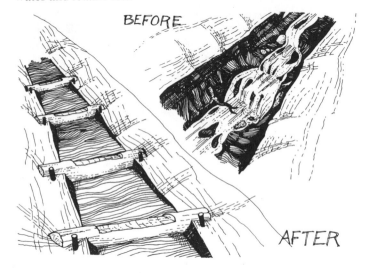

Steps should be thoughtfully placed on the trail to ensure that hikers will use them. They have to be in the most attractive place to walk and not too high; otherwise, they will be avoided by hikers. Hikers bypassing steps will soon create a new eroded route which others will use. Keep the rise to twelve inches or less as a general rule.

Even steps that are well-placed are avoided by some hikers, particularly if they are tired and going uphill. In order to prevent this, place dead wood or stones alongside the steps. Trails that are located in particularly wide gullies can be narrowed by placing scree on one or both sides, leaving the steps in the middle or along one edge. Sometimes a drainage ditch, usually on the uphill side of the trail, is needed to collect water and to channel it down alongside the steps to a waterbar, where it can be removed from the trail. Low and simple rock walls or bands of rubble might be needed alongside heavily used trails or in alpine zones. These rock walls, as well as brush and scree placed along the trail, may require annual repair as hikers, frost action, and water dislodge them, often depositing the materials on the trail tread itself. The object of placing such materials beside a trail is obviously to make walking off the trail difficult, thus containing traffic on a stabilized treadway. The maintainer should recognize that rock walls and piles of brush can greatly infringe on the primitive qualities of the trail environment. He should strive to make these measures as unobtrusive and natural-appearing as possible.

## Rock Steps

Rock steps are far more desirable than log steps, since they last longer and are much more pleasing aesthetically. Over time they will begin to look as if they were naturally in the trail, especially if they are placed carefully. Suitable rock may not be readily available in some locations; rock steps are so far superior to log ones, however, that the additional effort required to obtain building material is almost always justified. A search may be required, sometimes well off the trail. In other cases, rock may be partially buried under duff and leaf litter, requiring some excavation. Any shape of rock can be used; however, a large, flat-surfaced rock is much easier to work with and makes a more usable tread. As for size, rocks should probably weigh at least 50 to 100 pounds. Much larger rocks have been placed with success. Smaller rocks are more apt to work loose eventually. The weight alone will help keep a large rock in place.

ROCK STEPS CROSS-SECTION

The basic tools needed to build rock steps are a crowbar, pick mattock, and shovel. Sometimes a hand winch and chains are necessary, especially on very steep slopes.

In placing steps, either of wood or rock, it is generally best to work up from the bottom of a slope. This procedure makes it easier to determine the best step placement and the optimum mix of stabilization techniques. When installing rock steps on very steep slopes, overlapping is sometimes necessary. This makes it imperative to work from the bottom up.

The first task involves finding the rock to be used, preferably uphill of the work site and off the trail out of view. Moving the rock to the trail is the next task. Sometimes one person alone can maneuver a rock to the trail using a crowbar or muscle power, rolling, flipping, and sliding the rock along. Occasionally several people are required, some working with crowbars and others pushing with arms or legs. Pick mattocks can prove useful in such maneuvers, also. Logs used for steps can sometimes be carried under an arm or on a shoulder. Two people, one on each end, may find it easier.

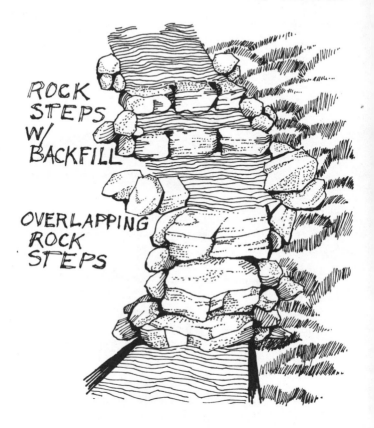

ROCK
STEPS
W/
BACKFILL

OVERLAPPING
ROCK
STEPS

Joint efforts must be carefully coordinated to prevent accidents, particularly pinched or crushed fingers. Some people wear leather gloves. Most, however, find it is less hazardous to use bare hands. With direct skin-to-rock contact the grip is generally better. Also, shifts in the rock can be felt more easily; thus, there is more warning and hands can be pulled clear faster. Though hands may take a beating at first due to the roughness of most stones, protective callouses soon develop.

**Barricades** — Working on steep slopes, AMC crews have sometimes built simple log barricades next to the trail and below where they are quarrying rock in the woods. By stacking some solid dead logs and a few freshly cut ones, a backstop into which rocks can be rolled can be created. In some cases barricades are built strictly on the chance that a rock may be lost in maneuvering it to the trail. Nothing is more frustrating than to spend a lot of time and sweat moving a rock, only to see it slip away and roll off out of sight down the slope. Barricades are also good for the safety of fellow workers and hikers. At all times, whether moving rock or logs, trail crews should use the utmost care and be conscious of hikers that may come by the work site.

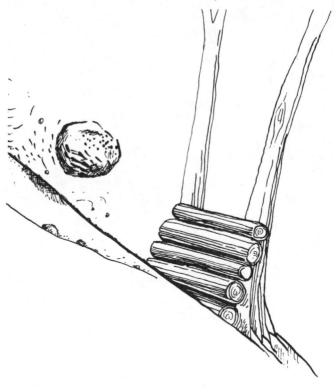

**Safety** — Unknowing hikers may stand in a particularly hazardous location and observe the work in progress. Watch for such bystanders and know where your fellow workers are, letting them know when you are attempting a difficult maneuver. Shout a warning if a rock goes out of control. Those working below should have escape routes planned or large trees or boulders picked out to step behind. It is wise to wear hard hats. In some cases it may be best to close a trail to hikers temporarily during construction. Limiting the number of crew working on a particular slope may also be wise. It is possible to have too many people and too much activity in one location.

Where there are boggy areas between rock sources and the trail, crews can sometimes make log skidways on which to slide the rock across the mud. Rolling through the mud, with its incredible suction power and the slipperiness it creates, can be extremely difficult, if not impossible.

**Equipment** — Winches and come-alongs with pieces of chain may prove valuable, and in some cases necessary, to move rock easily and safely, particularly on very steep terrain. Open-faced, two-ton cable winches and 10- to 20-foot lengths of ¼-inch chain with a slip hook on one end and a grab hook on the other are most commonly used. Chain falls, chain winches, and winches with enclosed casings sometimes do not work well, since dirt and debris get into the mechanisms, jamming them and requiring frequent maintenance. Use of hard hats and leather gloves is encouraged when working with winches and chains. Cables may develop very sharp splinters.

A number of hitches and wraps can be made with chain to enable the maintainer to flip a rock, spin it around, or drag it.

A crowbar is often necessary to lift a rock so a chain can be slipped in place under it. When pulling a rock across the ground, never let the winch alone do the work. Have someone wedge the leading edge up and unsnag it when it gets caught or digs into the ground. On a slope the crowbar handler should keep out of the area below the rock in case it should slip from its hitch.

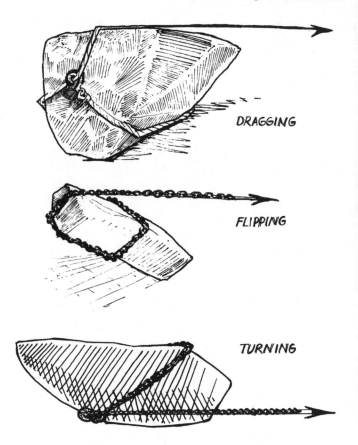

DRAGGING

FLIPPING

TURNING

Large trees can serve as anchors. Loop a short length of chain around the trunk with a piece of leather, rubber, or canvas as protection against chafing the bark. A large rock may also function as an anchor — or a stout log or crowbar wedged between rocks or trees may do the trick if the rock being pulled is not too large.

Never use "cheater" bars on a winch. Handles supplied with most winches are generally designed to bend for safety after a certain load limit is reached. Do not overstrain the winch or its cable or damage may result. Snapping cable can cause injury and a chain, if under enough tension, can also whip about.

Trail workers have used a winch, pulley, and chain to set up a cableway for moving rock in a manner similar to that used to move logs in some logging operations. With a gentle slope and a taut cable between two trees or other anchors, a rock can be slung underneath on a pulley and slid downhill or across the slope to the trail. Another moving method is to lower the rock downslope with one winch while a second winch, off to one side, pulls it across the slope. The second winch also serves as a backup for safety.

DONKEY WINCH

Chainsaw-powered "donkey" winches may prove practical for moving rock or logs in some cases. Horses, oxen, or machinery might be feasible, even necessary, to move large volumes of material at times. Generally they are not needed and are not appropriate in trail work due to the damage that may be done to the treadway.

**Placement** — After having maneuvered the rock to the trail, dig a hole to accommodate it. Before placing it in the hole, carefully look over the rock and figure which face is best placed up to provide the best step; then determine in which direction it should be turned for the most stability. Once a large rock is dropped into place it may be very difficult, especially if mud is present, to pull it back out and reset it. Be sure each rock step is securely placed. Stones should not shift at any point, even slightly. Proper placement requires skill, experience, and patience. When only small- and medium-sized rocks are available, several must sometimes be put side by side to provide a treadway of adequate width. Where thin, flat stones are found, it is usually best to place them on edge buried deep into the trail tread and with a slight uphill slope. The area behind and above the rock is then backfilled with soil and rubble. With an uphill slope, pressure from hikers' feet will push the rock into the slope rather than out and away from it.

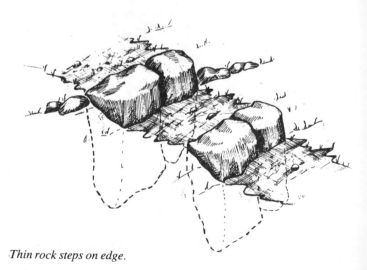

*Thin rock steps on edge.*

When rock steps are built on a steep slope, the rocks may need to be closely spaced, sometimes overlapping lower steps up to, or even more than, one-half their surface area. Overlapping large, flat rocks can add to the stability of the others in the steps. Smaller rocks should not be used to "wedge" a step that is unstable. Wedges will eventually work loose and the step may fall out. Each rock should be solidly fitted into the soil and onto steps below. When using overlapping stones, two or more contact points are required for stability.

For aesthetic reasons, and in some cases to allow for better drainage, it is best to avoid perfectly straight staircases up a slope. Put in some twists and bends for visual reasons. Drainage is often easier to construct at corners. Also, break up the "staircase effect" through use of odd-shaped but well-placed rock. Offset some steps rather than have them all in a direct line.

Rock steps may be used to assist hikers up steep, ledgy areas which have been bypassed, resulting in damage to soils and vegetation on the sides of the ledge. By stacking large rocks on top of each other and wedging them into any existing corners or cracks in the ledge, secure and attractive footing can be provided.

One very important aspect of rock step construction that some trail workers forget is provision for drainage. This usually results from a feeling that larger rocks will stay in place forever. Without good drainage, though, even the largest, most stable steps will eventually work loose as the soil around them washes away. Ice action will move steps, also.

**Clean-up** — After the rock work is completed, evidence of excavation and "skidder trails" developed during movement of the rock to the trail should be brushed in and holes filled with debris, dead wood, and leaf litter, particularly if close to the trail. Many heavily worked trails will look muddy or raw immediately after construction but will "wear in" over the course of a year or two, so that most hikers will not even realize that the trail has been reconstructed. Rock work has an advantage over wood here, since, when well-constructed, it can become practically invisible to the unpracticed eye.

## Wood Steps

The construction of wood steps is for the most part similar to building waterbars, except that steps are put in perpendicular to the trail and the uphill side of the log is backfilled and not trenched.

Spruce and fir are, again, the usual choices for wood; the diameter should be between six and twelve inches. On steeper slopes a larger diameter log gives more vertical rise. With small diameter stock, steps have to be very close together and more numerous to provide the desired vertical rise.

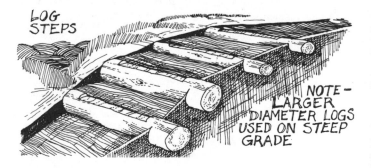

LOG STEPS

NOTE — LARGER DIAMETER LOGS USED ON STEEP GRADE

The length of the wood steps depends on the width of the trail. When placed in a gully, the ends of the logs should extend into the banks. Too short a step will allow water and people to go around, and it will not fully retain the soil.

The trench that the log is placed in should be roughly one-third the diameter of the log. The log is then set into the trench and secured with stakes similar to those described for waterbars.

Two stakes should be placed on the downhill side, one near each end, at an angle away from the log; they should be driven or cut flush. Large rocks on each end will suffice, also.

STEPS SHOULD FILL THE GULLY

LARGE ROCKS CAN BE USED IN THE PLACE OF STAKES

Once the log step is secure, the uphill side can be backfilled with soil removed when digging the trench. When steps are placed in a series, ideally the bottom of the upper log should be just a bit higher than the top of the lower log, with the soil in between slightly sloped. This will ensure a downhill slope and prevent puddling behind the step. As the rounded surface of the step can be slippery, the final touch is to slightly flatten the top of the log with an axe.

**Special Techniques** — In some cases where placing steps is not possible, more complex structures may be necessary. This usually occurs in very steep locations or along seriously gullied trails.

One such structure is what might be called a *combination ladder,* or a combination of cribbing and stepping. This technique is useful where a very steep slope or one with bedrock near the surface of the ground exists, making it difficult to secure regular steps.

It basically consists of building a log ladder and laying it into or up against the slope. Then each step is backfilled with gravel or rock scree. There should not be space behind the "rungs" which people might step into. Tops of the log "rungs" should be flattened with an axe.

"CRIB LADDER"
RUNGS FIT INTO NOTCHES
AND ARE SPIKED
STEPS ARE BACKFILLED
WITH ROCK AND SCREE

There are many possible variations of this technique. Ten- to twelve-inch spikes, ⅜″ in diameter, can be used to construct the log ladder.

Pinned wooden steps have been developed and used by local U.S. Forest Service staff to traverse difficult ledges that do not provide adequate foot and hand holds and that cannot be avoided through relocation. Pressure-treated wooden steps two feet long, produced by splitting six by eight inch stock from corner to corner, are attached to the ledge with foot-long steel bars set partially into the rock. A gas-powered jackhammer is used to drill the holes. A jackhammer can also be used to cut small steps into a ledge. Most maintainers agree that such high-standard techniques should be utilized only as a last resort to more conventional work or relocation due to the expense and difficulty, as well as for aesthetic reasons.

PINNED STEPS

## Rock and Log Cribbing

*Rock* and *log cribbing* are techniques that involve creating a treadway on sections of trail that have severe gullying, or when traversing a steep side slope.

Steps can be put in a gully, but in a severely eroded area steps alone will not solve the problem of continued erosion. It may be more desirable to remove the trail from the bottom of the gully by using cribs, or to relocate it completely away. On sidehill cuts, cribbing is often needed to stabilize the upper and lower slopes.

Rock cribbing, which is the most aesthetic as well as the most durable, can be used to strengthen the low or high side of a trail. On especially steep sidehill locations the treadway must sometimes be constructed in rock wall fashion.

ROCK CRIB CROSS SECTION

A log crib consists basically of a log securely positioned alongside the edge of the trail. The log should be at least ten inches in diameter and peeled. Length depends on the area, but generally a long, heavy log is best. The weight helps to hold it in place. It cannot be overemphasized that the log should be very secure, as it must support large amounts of soil and rock along with the weight of the passing hikers. It can be secured by large stakes or rocks, or butted up against rocks or trees. Logs perpendicular to the trail and notched and spiked into the crib log might be used as combination steps, spacers, and retainers.

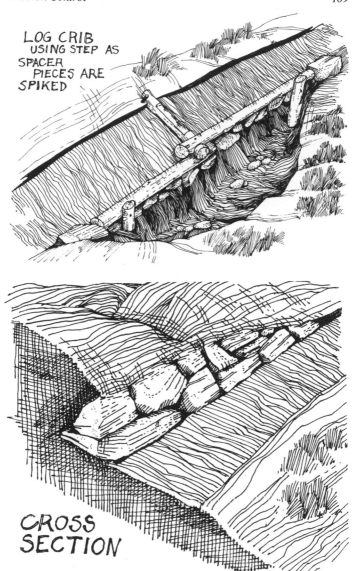

LOG CRIB
USING STEP AS
SPACER
PIECES ARE
SPIKED

CROSS
SECTION

The uphill side of the tread can be strengthened using log cribbing, which can be constructed in a number of ways, one of which is illustrated below.

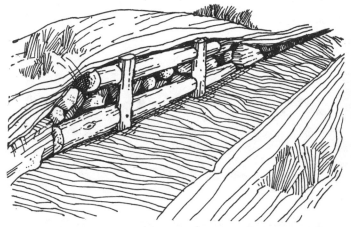

In constructing cribs or retainers for the lower side of the trail, one must keep in mind that the treadway should remain gently sloped to the outside or downhill side to ensure natural drainage. No crib or retainer should inhibit this drainage, nor should the treadway be flat or sloped toward the inside or uphill side of the treadway. Otherwise, water will puddle or flow along the tread.

When cribbing around a gully, fill in the gully afterward with rock and wood debris to reduce further erosion and prevent hikers from traveling there. Ideally, the gully will begin to fill with forest litter and will at least partially recover.

The Potomac Appalachian Trail Club sometimes uses an innovative method to deal with gullies; it involves filling the gully with alternating layers of brush, rock, leaf litter, and soil. Once the gully is filled and capped off with a healthy layer of soil, drainage to prevent the gully from reforming can be installed. Soil is obtained by digging small pits off the trail.

# 8

# HARDENING TRAILS IN WET AREAS

---

TRAILS IN FLAT, LOW-LYING, WET terrain, as well as mountain bogs with highly organic, wet soils, are frequently plagued by destruction of plants and surface soil horizons. Wet, slippery, muddy locations develop very quickly on these soils, causing puddling of water on the trail treadway. Hikers, wanting to keep their feet dry, walk to the side of the tread and so cause a vicious circle of soil breakdown and trail widening. There are a number of techniques that can be applied to trails in this situation that will help to stabilize the damaged soils and allow trailside plant life to recover.

Step stones, rock treadway, or bog bridges made of native wood are the most frequently used solutions in these situations. However, before these techniques are used the drainage of the area under consideration should be investigated. Relocation opportunities should also be checked out, especially if the wet area is extensive.

Wet, muddy locations frequently develop on trails because the treadway is lower than surrounding terrain. Water draining laterally through soils becomes trapped on the lower surfaces that make up the treadway. Rather than bridge trails in these situations, a better long-term solution is to drain the wet area in question, especially if it is small and has a low end which, once ditched, would permit water to flow off the trail. Many times what looks at first glance to be a low, flat section of trail will actually have a very moderate slope and therefore an imperceptible flow of water. Small "flowing" wet spots such as this should be drained with waterbars and drainage ditches. The feasibility of this technique should be investigated before resorting to step stones or bridges. Look for opportunities to relocate on to higher, drier ground, also.

If an area cannot be drained, or if for environmental reasons it should not be drained, and if relocation is not feasible, then trail hardening techniques should be used. These techniques offer dry passage for hikers and contain traffic on a hardened surface, thus allowing adjacent soils and plant life to reestablish themselves.

## Step Stones and Rock Treadway

If rock is available, it can be used to provide a longer-lasting and more aesthetic treadway than log bridges.

STEP STONE
TREAD
NOTE DRAINAGE
DITCH

*Step stones* are basically just rocks set into the mud so that a stable and spacious treadway is formed. Any size and shape of rock can be used. Of course, the larger ones are less prone to unwanted movement. Set them so the best surface for walking upon is presented.

Step stones should be stable and must not protrude too high above the ground surface nor be so low as to be inundated with mud and water. Otherwise, people are apt to avoid them.

A *rock treadway* is simply a more intensive use of rock than is the case with step stones. Many rocks are set side by side, or are set into what is called a "rock box." With a *rock box,* a frame is constructed of logs which are peeled and spiked together, and rock is used to fill in the interior. With particularly good, square rock such a frame is not needed, since the rocks can be laid in flagstone fashion.

Where rock is absent, log boxes can be made and filled with soil, though this is a very time-consuming process. Another technique is to dig drainage ditches on one or both sides of the tread, using soil from the ditch excavation to build up the tread. Do not be afraid to use wet and muddy soil, since it will dry out after a while.

"ROCK BOX"

*Rock treadway can be used in place of a bridge and, though more difficult to construct, it affords a more permanent solution.*

## Bog Bridges

In areas where rock is scarce, which is often the case in boggy locations, log bridges can be constructed to form a hardened tread.

These bridges can also be used to ford small streams and gullies. In either case they will provide a dry, stable treadway. Life expectancy of such bridges is usually ten years or greater depending on species of tree, wetness of location, and diameter and quality of wood used. Softwoods, such as cedar, hemlock, spruce, and fir, are the easiest to work with and last the longest.

Basically there are two types of bridges, topped log and split log. Both are relatively simple to construct, requiring only a few hand tools. A third — but not often used — type consists of bridge stringers* made by sawing a log in half with a chainsaw. This produces a flat surface but involves a great deal of wear and tear on the chainsaw and the operator. A large chainsaw with a ripping chain, requiring an experienced operator, is necessary.

Topped log bridges are the most durable, and therefore the best bridges to use. Because the stringers are topped and have only approximately one-third of their mass removed, this bridge is stronger and more impervious to water, and therefore to rot, than split log bridges. The stability gained from the extra weight of a topped log bridge is an added positive characteristic. Its major shortcoming is that it usually requires two full trees, which may make the split log bridge more feasible to install without running short of wood supplies on sparsely wooded areas. The split log bridge, in addition to being economical with wood, is lighter and therefore easier to transport to its final location. Of course, a split log bridge requires larger diameter timber; with a topped log bridge one can use smaller logs.

*Stringers are longitudinal parts of a bridge forming the treadway.

*Log bridge*

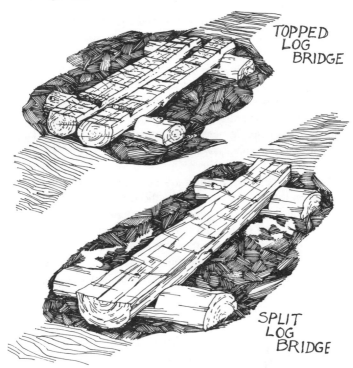

TOPPED LOG BRIDGE

SPLIT LOG BRIDGE

**Topped Log Bridges** — A sharp axe is the main tool necessary in constructing a topped log bridge. A small chainsaw, if available, can make the work easier and faster. A peeler or bark spud greatly facilitates peeling, and a sledgehammer is best for driving spikes. Digging tools such as a mattock and shovel facilitate placing base logs.

With smaller diameter logs used for topped log bridge stringers, usually two are needed side by side to provide a treadway of adequate width. Stringers should be no less than six inches in diameter; the average length should be around eight to ten feet. Logs should be peeled to retard rot.

The base logs alone can be notched and the stringers set into them, or corresponding notches in both the stringers and base logs can be used. However, the stringers will be stronger if they are not notched. The ends of the stringers should not overhang the base log by more than six to eight inches. Too much overhang can break off or tip up the bridge when it is stepped on. Base logs are generally three to four feet long and eight to ten inches in diameter. Where it is extremely wet and muddy, larger base logs may be necessary for stability.

Once the base log notches are cut, the two stringers can be placed on them. A space between the stringers should be left to prevent debris from collecting and rotting the wood. It should, however, be no more than two to three inches, so that a foot cannot slip down between them. A fairly uniform width can be achieved by alternating the butt ends of the stringers. The stringers should be level or, if sloped at all, sloped slightly to the inside.

Some top the logs in the woods to avoid having to clean chips on the trail. Others top them before spiking them to the base logs. If untopped stringers are to be anchored to the base logs before topping, a small notch roughly two inches square and two inches deep must be cut in the top of each stringer to accept the spikes. (Spikes ten inches by three-eighths inch are recom-

SPIKE IN THROUGH
THE NOTCHES
STRINGERS
2 – 3" APART

mended to nail the unit together.) Notches allow the spikes to be countersunk so they will not be hit when topping is done. Spikes should be angled slightly in opposite directions to provide tension to hold the stringers more securely in place.

TOPPING

CHAINSAW CUTS MADE 6-8" APART PIECES THEN SPLIT OFF — MAKE SURE THE SURFACE ISN'T CANTED

After the stringers are spiked securely, their tops can be flattened with an axe or an adze by hewing the upper surfaces. With a chainsaw it can be done more easily and quickly. Vertical cuts are made with the chainsaw roughly every six inches and to a depth one-third of the way through the log. Then, using an axe or an adze, the top can be chipped off flat.

PLACE BRIDGES NO MORE THAN 6" APART. ENDS OF STRINGERS SHOULDN'T TOUCH THE BANKS

When topping stringers already spiked, the major thing to be careful about is that the bridge surface does not end up sloped to one side.

**Split Log Bridges** — Split log bridges require the use of three primary tools: a single-bit axe, an eight- to ten-pound sledgehammer, and four four- to six-pound steel splitting wedges. A peeler or bark spud, if available, greatly facilitates peeling, though an axe alone will do.

The diameter of a log to be split should be no less than ten inches. Length is up to the builder, but usually eight- to ten-foot stringers are used. Generally spruce or fir is used, since this wood is easy to cut, peel, and split. The trees are also relatively lightweight, which aids when carrying them. Hardwoods split fairly well but are very heavy, hard to cut and peel, and do not last as long.

In choosing trees to cut, look for ones that are the straightest and most uniform in diameter. Also look for trees with the fewest branches, which usually means fewer knots to contend with when splitting. Do not use trees with "heart rot."

Once the log to be split is felled, it must then be peeled. Though the peeled log can be a bit slippery to handle, the spiral of the grain and location of knots is then visible. Also, during the splitting process the split can easily be seen and corrected should it begin to angle off to one side.

The next step is to look over the log and choose a line of split. If there are many knots, try to pick a line that will go between them if possible. The splitting process itself is begun by driving the axe into the center of one end. It is often easiest and best to begin at the larger diameter end. This initial end split will provide a good, straight starting split from which you can work, lengthening it until the log is split in half.

Next, drive a wedge into the top of the log in line with and near the starting split. As you drive in the wedge the split will lengthen. Drive the wedge in until only the top two to three inches is showing, or until the split begins to spiral off to one side.

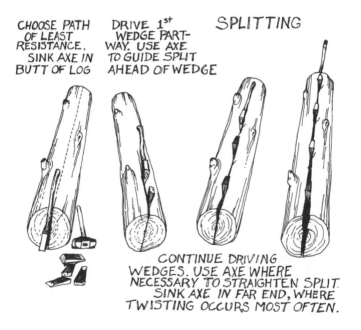

CHOOSE PATH OF LEAST RESISTANCE. SINK AXE IN BUTT OF LOG

DRIVE 1st WEDGE PARTWAY. USE AXE TO GUIDE SPLIT AHEAD OF WEDGE

SPLITTING

CONTINUE DRIVING WEDGES. USE AXE WHERE NECESSARY TO STRAIGHTEN SPLIT. SINK AXE IN FAR END, WHERE TWISTING OCCURS MOST OFTEN.

If spiraling occurs, take the axe and carefully make several chops to bring the split back in line; then drive the wedge in farther. Be careful not to hit the axe blade or handle or your knuckles on the wedge.

Continue to alternately drive wedges and chop in between them until you reach the end of the log. If four wedges are not enough, leave the first one in place and remove the middle ones, driving them in leapfrog fashion beyond the last one. As you near the end, drive the axe into the butt to ensure a straight end split.

The log should now be almost completely split in half, held together by a few resistant strands on the bottom side. Remove two wedges and leave two in, one near each end; then roll the log over. Using the two wedges and your axe, finish the split. Be careful not to let the stringers splinter where they are held by resistant strands, or they may be weakened or left with a twist. Cut off any large loose splinters.

NOTCHING
NOTE - 2 POINTS OF CONTACT ON SIDES OF STRINGER

HERE, THERE IS A GAP TO ONE SIDE. THIS WILL ROCK.

Attach these stringers to base logs in the same way as it is done for a topped log bridge.

After the bridge is spiked together, look at the surface of the stringer. If it has a ridge in one spot or is twisted, use the axe to flatten it out. Do not hit the spikes!

ANGLE THE SPIKES IN OPPOSITE DIRECTIONS

**Bridge Construction Reminders** — Whether you build a split log or topped log bridge, in order for it to be effective it must be used by the hiker. Make sure that the treadway width is sufficient to make walking on it easy. In some cases it may be necessary to use double stringers, two side by side — or in the case of particularly thin stock, three in parallel.

The treadway should not be tilted or angled to one side, nor should the bridge be unstable, rocking, or very springy. With stringers that are over eight to ten feet long or that are very springy, use three or more base logs for support. It is probably best to keep bridges short and therefore stable. Shorter bridges are easier to work with, also.

The height of the bridge surface should not be over eight to ten inches from the ground. A high bridge is hard to step up onto or off of, and can be difficult to traverse for those averse to heights. Dig in the base logs if the unit will be too high or if it is unstable.

Also, a stable rocky or dry soil should be found at the end of a bridge, not mud or slippery roots. When bridges are placed end to end, a space of no more than six inches should separate them.

Caution should be exercised when bridging on pond shores or in any areas that are prone to flooding in wet seasons. If water levels rise substantially, bridges will float and drift off the trail. This might happen, for instance, along a pond shore that has beaver activity. Trails in these situations might best be relocated rather than bridged.

# 9

# STREAM CROSSINGS

---

ALMOST ALL TRAILS, SOMEWHERE in their routing, cross one or more streams. In some cases a stream is one of the major natural features of a trail route.

Whether or not any hiker aid is necessary at a stream crossing depends upon the type of use expected, the season of use, and the nature of the stream and crossing. Hiker safety is the primary consideration. Convenience may or may not be important. In a remote backcountry area, hopping from stone to stone and the possibility of getting wet feet are part of the experience. On the other hand, on an urban nature trail used by a wide variety of people, many in street shoes and with little hiking experience, convenience may be important. A trail crossing that does not require a bridge in the summer for hikers may need one for skiers in the winter. Requirements during normal low stream flows may be quite different from those during spring thaw. Some streams are also prone to unexpected flash floods, with water levels and current changing dramatically; in such cases a bridge may be required.

Where possible natural stream crossings or fords are best. These may be enhanced through the placement of step stones. This will work only where stream flow is low and does not fluctuate; otherwise, the step stones will be washed away. Also, the stream bottom must be solid for this bridging method to be effective.

For small stream crossings of ten to fifteen feet in width, simple log puncheon or bog bridges (see Chapter 8) may suffice. A single large stringer with two base logs may work. Generally double stringers are best, since they provide better footing. Bridges three feet high or higher above the stream, or those over a fast current, should probably have a hand rail.

TWO STRINGER WITH RAIL

Occasionally stream banks may be uneven, requiring a gently sloped bridge or a log crib on the low side to raise it up. On a sloped bridge, small steps can be cut in the stringers or pieces of log or wood may be nailed to the top of the stringers, in chicken walk fashion, for traction. We have also heard of maintainers who have coated the logs with tar and thrown sand onto them, others have nailed chicken wire or mesh fencing to the stringer tops, securing the loops at close intervals.

Before bridging larger streams, the maintainer should make sure the crossing is necessary. Sometimes a crossing can be eliminated through a different trail route. If a crossing must be made, it should be determined whether or not the present location is the best one. Occasionally, a ford can be found elsewhere or a crossing requiring a smaller bridge can be located. Evidence of stream erosion should be noted and such sites avoided. The straighter stretches of stream are the most stable. Stream bends tend to erode at the outside.

Flood levels should be determined in advance, also. Look for evidence of the high water mark in the form of scraped bark on stream bank trees and deposits of stream debris. Consult local residents for observations and the Soil Conservation Service for stream flow and flood level data. Other government agencies and officials may have this information on hand, too. In some cases a flood overflow channel may exist. A larger bridge or extension may be required to span it. Otherwise, any steps or access ramp in the overflow channel may be washed away periodically and will need replacement.

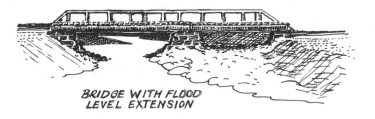

BRIDGE WITH FLOOD
LEVEL EXTENSION

## Building Single Span Stringer Bridges

Single span wooden bridges, made of native materials or milled timber, are the most common large bridges on trails. If both stream banks are high enough to keep the stringer's well above the flood level, extensive cribbing is not necessary. The stringers can be secured to a single base log or sill on each end, using 10- or 12-inch spikes or large bolts. To prevent rot the base log should be placed on flat stone or ledge. Drift pins sometimes can be used to hold the base log in place, though the weight of the bridge itself is generally sufficient.

Base logs, as well as the rest of the bridge, should be of rot-resistant wood such as hemlock, locust, spruce, larch, or Douglas fir. Remove all bark. Wood treatments lengthen the life of the bridge. Logs should be dry to facilitate application of preservatives. Avoid getting wood preservatives into the stream, however.

Sometimes one stream bank is low and a crib is needed to get the bridge high enough at one end so that the tread is relatively level. In other locations, cribs or piers may be necessary at both ends. Stone piers require a great deal of effort and the skill of a mason. Additionally, they may be out of place in some settings.

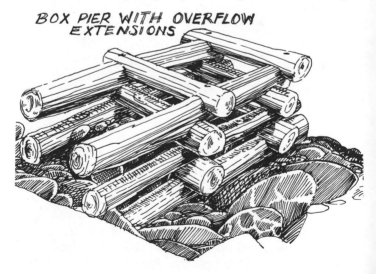

BOX PIER WITH OVERFLOW EXTENSIONS

*Gabiens,* wire cages filled with stone, may also be used. They are not very aesthetic, however. Log cribs are most commonly used.

BOX PIER

All cribs are constructed of logs, eight to ten inches in diameter. Notches, cut with an axe or chainsaw on the underside of each log, prevent water from collecting and reduce rot. Drift pins or 10- to 12-inch 3/8-inch diameter spikes are used to hold them together.

Rock is placed within the crib to add mass and strength. Using rock gathered nearby or from the stream, fill the crib as you construct it. It is easier than having to lift rock up over the highest log after it is all built. Since removing stones from the stream channel may facilitate water flow, larger rocks can be pushed or pulled to each side of the stream and placed along the bases of the cribs, particularly on the upstream side, for added protection.

After the crib has been built high enough, the stringer can be secured to it using large spikes or galvanized bolts. The size of the stringer depends upon the type of wood and length of the span. Below is a chart for determining the appropriate diameter, in most cases, for both logs and rough-sawn timber.

## BEAM SPAN TABLE

| | | SINGLE BEAM | | DOUBLE BEAM | |
|---|---|---|---|---|---|
| | BEAM SIZE | Maximum Span | Maximum Cantilever | Maximum Span | Maximum Cantilever |
| Round Beams — Diameter | 4″ | 6′ | 2′ | 8″ | 3″ |
| | 5″ | 9′ | 3′ | 12′ | 4′ |
| | 6″ | 12′ | 4′ | 14′ | 5′ |
| | 7″ | 15′ | 5′ | 18′ | 6′ |
| | 8″ | 18′ | 6′ | 22′ | 7′ |
| | 9″ | 21′ | 8′ | 25′ | 8′ |
| | 10″ | 25′ | 9′ | 29′ | 9′ |
| | 12″ | 32′ | 10′ | 37′ | 12′ |
| | 14″ | 39′ | 11′ | 45′ | 13′ |
| | 16″ | 47′ | 14′ | 54′ | 16′ |
| | 18″ | 55′ | 16′ | 63′ | 18′ |
| Rectangular Beams — Width × Depth | 4″ × 4″ | 8′ | 3′ | 10′ | 4′ |
| | 4″ × 4″ | 12′ | 4′ | 15′ | 5′ |
| | 4″ × 8″ | 17′ | 5′ | 20′ | 6′ |
| | 6″ × 4″ | 10′ | 3′ | 12′ | 4′ |
| | 6″ × 6″ | 15′ | 5′ | 17′ | 6′ |
| | 6″ × 8″ | 20′ | 6′ | 23′ | 8′ |
| | 6″ × 10′ | 25′ | 8′ | 29′ | 10′ |
| | 6″ × 12′ | 30′ | 10′ | 35′ | 12′ |
| | 8″ × 4″ | 11′ | 4′ | 13′ | 4′ |
| | 8″ × 6″ | 17′ | 6′ | 19′ | 6′ |
| | 8″ × 8″ | 22′ | 7′ | 25′ | 8′ |
| | 10″ × 4″ | 12′ | 4′ | 14′ | 5′ |
| | 10″ × 6″ | 18′ | 6′ | 21′ | 7′ |
| | 10″ × 8″ | 24′ | 8′ | 28′ | 9′ |
| | 10″ × 10′ | 30′ | 10′ | 34′ | 11′ |
| | 10″ × 12′ | 36′ | 12′ | 41′ | 13′ |

From the *Trail Manual of the Florida Trail*

*Three stringer with handrail*

Due to their length and weight, stringers can be hard to carry and maneuver into position. Timber carriers may help. Several block and tackles or hand winches, with extra lengths of cable or chain, along with crowbars, can greatly facilitate the task. Small lengths of log can be placed underneath stringers to provide rollers, as the Egyptians did for moving stone blocks centuries ago. Horses or small tractors might be used, where appropriate, in some easily accessible locations. Once at the site, most builders try to get the stringer in place across the stream, with the ends beside each sill or crib; then they lift it into place. Ramps made of logs and placed against the side of a crib can also help get the stringer up on top.

Decking, made from small-diameter (four to six inches) logs, larger logs split in half, or rough-cut timber two inches thick, goes on next. It is possible to simply have two or more stringers, hewn or adzed flat on the top for good footing, to provide an adequate treadway, if the stringers are close together. Generally, though, decking is best. Small spaces, one-half to one inch wide, should be left between deck pieces to allow for drainage. Before putting decking on, some builders place tar paper or aluminum flashing over the top of the stringers for drainage and to prevent rot. If the bridge is over a fast current or three feet or more above the stream, a secure railing should be added to one or both sides. In some instances, several steps or a small ladder are required on each end due to the height of the cribs. Where access is easy and the use of non-native material is appropriate, pressure-treated telephone poles can be used for stringers. Pressure-treated lumber can also be used for the decking and railings.

To prevent loss of the bridge during floods, cable one end of the stringers to a large tree, boulder, or other anchor. If washed loose, one end will float free and the bridge will end up against the stream bank. If you cable both sides, the bridge may stay in place but collect debris and eventually succumb completely to the force of the flood. Do not underestimate the power of a flooding stream.

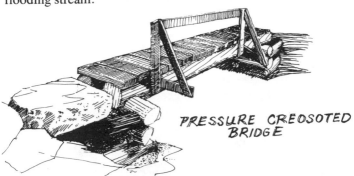

PRESSURE CREOSOTED BRIDGE

## Other Designs

The load capacity of fixed stringers generally limits spans to forty feet or less. A longer distance can be bridged using a midstream center crib and two spans. This will work only where flood levels are low and flow is slow; otherwise, the center crib may be destroyed.

*Bridge with center crib*

Most stream crossings of forty feet or more require specially designed bridges, such as a laminated timber bridge (10 to 90 feet, but 60 feet practically), a steel girder bridge (up to 60 feet practically), a prefabricated steel bridge (20 to 168 inches), a web joist bridge (about 100 feet), or a timber suspension bridge (up to 200 feet). These are all extremely expensive, ranging in total cost from $5,000 to $40,000. They also require the expertise of engineers and experienced builders to install them.

TENSION BRIDGE

*Wood laminated bridge*

Where stream crossings are large and unavoidable, requiring an expensive bridge, be sure an existing trail or road bridge nearby cannot be utilized. Sometimes it is best to consider relocating a trail rather than tackle such a large, expensive project.

If you are interested in history and a bridge other than a native log style will be in keeping with the nature of the trail, you might consider a kingpost, queenpost, or other type of truss bridge. All precursors of the well-known covered bridge, these simple designs work well when dealing with spans of from 15 to 20 feet on up to 75 feet or more. Operation L.I.V.E. (Learning In Vigorous Environments), an outing and experimental learning group at Keene (New Hampshire) State College, designed and built a beautiful thirty-foot kingpost bridge for a local trail.

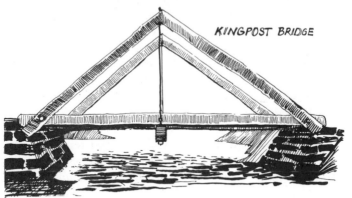

KINGPOST BRIDGE

The original kingpost trusses were prone to ice and flood damage, since they were underneath the stringers. Eventually someone realized that the principle of the triangle, which will hold its shape under pressure, would work just as well on top of the bridge. The queenpost design allowed a longer span and more complex designs using multiple trusses and arches to further lengthen the distance that could be bridged. Research

into the history of covered bridges will prove valuable if someone is interested in such designs. For the mortise and tenon
joints commonly used, look into one of the many good books
available on post and beam construction.

The Maine Appalachian Trail Club and local snowmobile
clubs utilize the principle of the kingpost bridge in their designs,
often using a combination of native logs and cable. Another
version uses a cable underneath to strengthen long stringers.

## Special Stream Crossing Devices

Cableways are sometimes used for stream crossings as an
alternative to bridging. In a few places small cable cars capable
of carrying one person can be found. The hiker hops in, grabs a
secondary cable, and pulls himself across. A second hiker pulls
back the car and repeats the process. In other situations two
cables are simply spaced one above the other and the hikers,
with feet on the lower one and hands on the upper, slide-step
across. Neither system is easy to use for most people, especially
if there are large packs or young children and pets in the
company.

Looking back into the past, current-driven ferries or rafts
running along one or two cables might be another alternative for
larger streams.

Where large bodies of water must be crossed, bridges built on
pilings may be the answer. Alternatively, floating bridges can
be constructed using blocks of styrofoam, as is the case with
liferafts and docks. Anchor cables should be placed to keep such
a bridge stable and in position. Use rot-resistant wood, and
make sure all hardware is galvanized or plated. AMC research

has shown that years ago floating bridges were sometimes built for wagons and cars; they utilized wooden barrels, hot-dipped in tar to seal them, underneath a frame and decking. You can consult a local dock builder for advice on pilings and styrofoam for such uses.

*Bridge on piling*

## Planning for Other Uses

In some locations snowmobiles or trailbikes may use a bridge, which can be undesirable from the hiker's standpoint. Build narrow bridges or have barricades at each end of the bridge to prevent this. Where large wildlife or farm animals are present, gates or stiles may be necessary to prevent access. If such crossings of the bridge are to be allowed, plan the carrying capacity of the structure with more weight in mind.

Suspension bridges that are easily accessible, particularly near the roadside, should probably have extra anti-sway cables attached to each side. Groups of children may try to see how much they can make the bridge flex up and down and from side to side. While it may be the goal in some instances to have a high-visibility bridge, in other cases screening by the use of landscaping and plantings may be desirable.

## Assistance

The U.S. Forest Service seems to have the most experience with and information on various designs of trail bridges. The National Park Service, state parks, and others may also be able to provide advice. Local engineers, contractors, and the telephone and power companies may be able to give guidance as well, in addition to being sources for hardware and cable. Sometimes local National Guard units are willing to take on public service projects, and may be able to provide labor in addition to technical help. Check also with other trail clubs and trail hiker and snowmobile organizations for information.

## Maintenance

An annual inspection should be made of all bridges and other stream crossings. Perform regular maintenance and replace materials as needed. All wood should be checked for soundness and painted or treated with preservative if required. Loose decking or railings should be fixed. Any cables, steel beams, or hardware should be painted with rust-resistant paint. Having a blueprint and pictures of each structure on file will greatly aid in repair work.

## Stream Crossings on Ski Touring Trails

Natural stream crossings are best, if possible, since there is no effort or expense required on the part of the maintainer, as there is in the construction and upkeep of bridges. Such crossings are generally best where the stream is slow and not too deep. Here water is more likely to freeze early in the winter and remain frozen longer. Also, if the water is shallow, the hazard to skiers is less in the event that they break through the ice. Gently sloped stream banks should be sought because they provide an easier crossing.

While there may be sufficient snow cover to ski on a trail, stream crossings, even small ones, may not yet have frozen or may have opened up during a thaw, preventing skiing. To lengthen the ski season, bridges may be necessary. In terms of construction, the same basic principles generally apply to ski trail bridges as to foot bridges. One major difference, however, is width. To hold snow and to compensate for crowning, a ski touring bridge should be four to six feet wide. To help retain snow, a curb can be made on each edge with small-diameter logs. If any grooming equipment is to be used on the trail, all bridges must be sufficiently strong to support the added weight.

CROWN + CURB ON X-COUNTRY
SKI BRIDGE

Since it is under the snow, the decking of a ski trail bridge does not need to provide good footing and be as tight as a foot bridge. The decking can be made from small-diameter logs, split logs, or rough planking. To fill in large spaces between pieces of decking and to hold snow, softwood boughs or hay can be used. Snow fence may work, also. Lay the boughs upside down or otherwise the ends will curve upward and stick out of the snow. Decking should be perpendicular to the direction of skier travel. If it is parallel a ski may slip down into the space between. If parallel stringers without decking are to be used alone, boughs or hay should definitely be added. A lumber walkway can be placed down the center if a ski trail bridge receives summer traffic.

Each end of a ski trail bridge should be graded and smooth. Skiers must not be able to catch ski tips on the exposed end of a bridge or its stringers. If height must be gained, a ramp may be necessary. Another method to gain height is simply to fill in a low spot with logs or brush, corduroy fashion.

WET AREAS

TRAIL

TRAIL

CORDUROY WITH LOGS    OR TOP WITH HAY    OR TOP WITH BOUGHS

A bridge three feet up or higher should have a hand railing on at least one side and generally on both. When on skis balance is often precarious. Be sure to allow for snow depth when determining the railing height. Do not leave railing ends protruding, especially if skiers will be traveling with any speed when crossing. Tapered railings are safest.

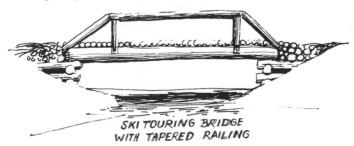

SKI TOURING BRIDGE WITH TAPERED RAILING

If the approach to a bridge involves slope that will propel the skier at any speed, it may be best not to have railings unless the bridge is very high. A crash into a railing can break skis, poles, and bones. A tumble off one edge of a bridge into snow may be less hazardous.

To develop and maintain good snow cover on a bridge, some effort is usually involved. Shoveling and packing snow onto the deck after the first snowfall can result in a better and more complete base. Later in the winter the snow will begin to melt and recede inward from the edges of the bridge, leaving the track on a high, narrow bank of snow in the middle. This is because the dark, exposed edges of the decking warm quickly in the sunlight and the center, being packed by skis all winter, is more dense and resistant to melting. To counteract this effect such a snow ridge should be broken down and scattered across the decking or more snow can be shoveled onto the edges. Some maintainers leave a snow shovel hanging on the bridge or a nearby tree for such work.

Where ski trails cross shallow wet or boggy areas, which may freeze late or thaw early, an alternative to bridging is the placement of boughs, hay, or log corduroy. For trail drainage, culverts generally work best. Waterbars tend to create mounds in the trail, and they thaw out, leaving an open ditch on the uphill side to traverse. Small bridges may be required over waterbars and drainage ditches where this is a problem.

Avoid crossings of bogs, ponds, and lakes, since they can be dangerous when the ice is thin. Provide alternate routes if water crossings are part of a trail.

# 10

# STILES

---

Trails, particularly those traversing private lands in urban and agricultural areas, sometimes must pass over or through fences. To prevent damage to fences and to eliminate the inevitable gate that someone forgot to close, both of which create landowner conflict, as well as to facilitate passage of hikers, stiles can be used. Stiles allow pedestrian travel and in most cases prevent passage of farm animals as well as off-road vehicles.

Milled lumber can be used to construct stiles in easily reached locations or where native materials are scarce or absent. Use two-inch or larger stock for strength. Rough cut lumber, having slightly larger dimensions than fully milled lumber, is strongest. Wood treated with preservatives will last longer. Railings or other parts touched by hikers should be treated with preservatives which will not stain or burn them. All nails, bolts, and hardware should be plated or galvanized.

If fences are electrified to contain animals, sections near stiles that people might touch can be covered with a piece of rubber hose. Slit it the entire length so it can be slipped over the wire. Hose can also be used to cover sections of barbed wire that hikers might get caught on when crossing over.

Below are several stile designs often used.

*Rail stile*

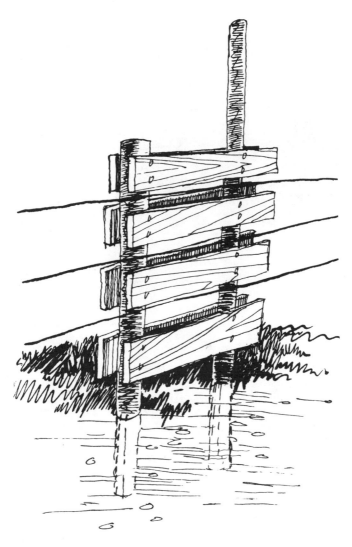

*Ladder stile*

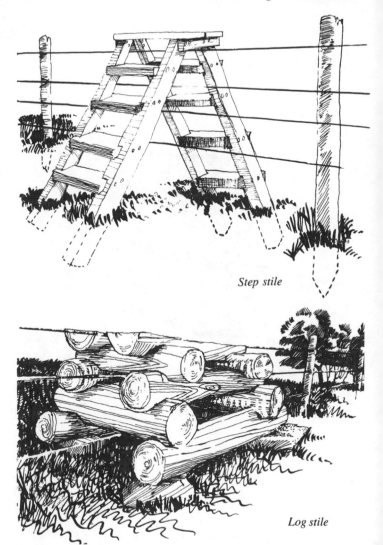

*Step stile*

*Log stile*

It is possible to make stiles completely out of native materials. This may be preferable at remote locations where native materials are abundant and where it would be too difficult to import finished materials. Rot-resistant tree species such as hemlock, spruce, or locust should be used. To prevent rot, bark should be removed and any portions of logs buried in the ground should be treated with wood preservative if possible.

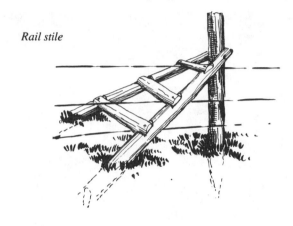

*Rail stile*

*Buried log stile*

Passage through a fence, rather than over it, can also be accommodated. A turnstile is one method. Where farm animals might go under or through a turnstile, a walk-through stile may be necessary. The tight turn and narrow space keep most farm animals from getting through. To contain smaller farm animals, a low step, barrier board, or hinged gate may be needed in the middle.

*Turnstile*

*Walk-through stile*

   With stone walls it is possible to make a narrow opening for hikers. A stone staircase up one side and down the other is also feasible, of course, but requires a great deal of work.

*Stone wall stile*

# 11

# DESIGN, CONSTRUCTION, AND MANAGEMENT OF CROSS COUNTRY SKI TOURING TRAILS

WITH THE INTRODUCTION OF LIGHT WEIGHT, high-quality equipment in recent years, cross country skiing has witnessed tremendous growth in popularity. An inexpensive recreational activity which can be enjoyed by all with or without formal ski touring facilities, the sport has found many new advocates since the mid-1970's, with use nearly doubling every year in the U.S. Some users have been refugees from crowded downhill slopes and the high cost of alpine skiing.

There are basically four types of cross country skiing experiences: racing or competitive skiing and recreational skiing, both on developed trails with a high standard of maintenance (i.e., grooming, tracking), and recreational skiing on primitive trails (i.e., backcountry touring not involving trails). When backcountry skiing requires the use of specialized alpine equipment or techniques in rough mountain areas, it is commonly known as ski mountaineering.

Bushwhack or backcountry touring and ski mountaineering do not involve the development of trails and thus will not be further discussed in this chapter. Opportunities for such skiing exist nearly everywhere and in all degrees of difficulty, from a ski out through the back woodlot to a major mountaineering trip into remote wildlands. Such experiences are not the primary ones that most cross country skiers seek.

At the other end of the spectrum is competitive skiing and recreational skiing on developed, high standard trails; this type of touring has the most participants and has seen the most growth to date. The private sector, primarily, has worked hard to meet the demands for this kind of touring experience. Witness the tremendous increase in the number of private touring centers on both private and public lands. Continued growth is expected.

In between is the recreational touring experience on primitive, low standard trails. Primarily the public sector, through various local, state, and federal agencies, has been involved in this area. At present such ski touring experiences are generally limited, however, and use is moderate. Demand in this area is expected to increase dramatically, though, in the near future. As ski tourers become more experienced and skilled, and as the developed, high standard trail facilities become increasingly crowded, more will seek the challenging, less used primitive trails. Such skiers, while not interested in grooming and set tracks, do wish to have marked, clear, and easily followed trails. Some will seek such trails, which are generally free, to avoid use fees usually associated with developed, high standard trail systems.

The Appalachian Mountain Club trails program maintains approximately twenty miles of ski touring trails in the Pinkham Notch area of the White Mountains; some additional touring trails are maintained elsewhere by chapters and camps of the Club. All are non-fee and primitive in nature, being ungroomed and unpatrolled. The Club wholly supports such ski touring opportunities as part of a spectrum of backcountry experiences. It hopes to develop more such opportunities and feels that others, particularly in the public sector, could and should do more to fill this niche.

## Planning and Design

There are a number of factors to take into consideration when planning a ski touring trail or trail network. First, review Chapters 1 and 2 of this book for the general factors involved in hiking trail design. Additionally, there are specific considerations for ski touring trails.

Development of a cross country ski trail system should begin with a determination of who will use the trails, their experience level, expected number of users, and whether or not it will be weekend use, day use, or evening use. A decision will be needed as to whether or not the maintaining organization will cater to one type of ski touring experience and level of expertise or to all. To some extent the land base will also affect this decision (i.e., rough terrain may preclude novice trails).

Standard trail degree-of-difficulty ratings used by many organizations are as given below. The ratings are determined by trail gradient, alignment, and width, assessed during normal or average snow conditions. A ski touring system should ideally have approximately 50% of the trails rated as easiest for novice use, approximately 30% with a more difficult rating for intermediate skiers, and 20% most difficult trails for expert skiers. There will certainly be constraints affecting these percentages in the form of trail location, terrain, and land management goals and objectives.

## TRAIL SIGNS

### Easiest

A green circle on white background, with white wavy stripe bisecting the green circle. The word "easiest" is below the circle. This designation is used on the area's easiest trails.

### More Difficult

A blue square on white background, with a more pronounced, white wavy stripe bisecting the square. The words "more difficult" are below the square. This designation is used on the area's trails that fall between "easiest" and "most difficult."

### Most Difficult

A black diamond on white background, with a white zig-zag stripe bisecting the diamond. The words "most difficult" are below the diamond. This designation is used on the area's most difficult trails.

### Caution

A red exclamation mark enclosed by a red triangle, on yellow background, with the word "caution" below the triangle.

### Grooming Equipment Warning Sign

A warning sign and the following lettering, in red on yellow background: "Warning! Grooming machines and maintenance personnel may be on the trails at any time."

From *NSTOA Operation Manual* © 1979

Assess other ski touring opportunities available in the region to see if there are gaps that can be filled, so that duplication can be minimized. Consideration may also be given to connecting with existing trails or areas to provide larger networks.

Efforts should be made to evaluate other recreational activities and land management practices in the area which might pose conflicts, so steps can be taken to minimize problems through trail layout and design. For example, snowmobiles and ski tourers, generallly incompatible groups, should be separated for aesthetic and safety reasons. While ski tourers may not detrimentally affect the experience of snowmobilers, the presence of snowmobiles may negatively impact the quality of the ski tourer's experience. Timber management activities − in terms of timing, use of roads by machinery which may also be used by ski tourers, and aesthetics − should also be reviewed. Ski touring may be incompatible with some wildlife areas, such as deer yards, because of stress placed on the animals due to human presence and compaction of routes that may be used by dogs that may chase the deer.

Accessibility to the public should be reviewed thoroughly, considering existing and potential roads, parking, public transportation, and winter snow removal. Snow removal must be coordinated with highway authorities or municipalities. Roads and parking should be designed to facilitate easy, efficient snow removal.

Once the potential types of trail experiences — and those to be catered to — have been assessed, information/education needs as well as sanitation facilities, search and rescue operations, and skier conveniences such as ski rental and repair, lodging, and meal accommodations, should be evaluated. Maintenance and management capabilities should be reviewed also.

Opportunities for further expansion should be assessed, as well as possibilities for future changes in operations, such as the addition of warming shelters or the beginning of grooming. Any construction should be done with the possibility of operational changes in mind — for instance, construction of bridges might allow for the passage of grooming equipment if it is likely that grooming might eventually be done.

## Trail Layout

The best time to lay out ski touring trails is in the late fall or winter when leaves are off the trees, creating better visibility. Before venturing out, consult maps and aerial photos to get a feel for the lay of the land and location of features. Be aware of the general trail layout considerations outlined in Chapter 3, as well as the factors specific to ski touring described here.

Laying out a trail in winter while on skis can be both fun and an effective way to actually test the skiability of the route. Another advantage in laying out trails with snow on the ground is that you can see where you have been by the tracks; thus, you do not have to use flagging tape as much to mark your travels. Caution should be exercised, however, as brush sticking out of the snow, limbs hanging down, and "spruce traps" are all hazards.

You should scout the route with another person, particularly in winter, for safety reasons and because two opinions are generally better than one. Two or more people can also cover more ground. Covering an area by traversing back and forth before homing in on a particular route can result in finding a natural feature that would be good to include or locating an old logging road that you were unaware of. Walk or ski any routes in both uphill and downhill directions to thoroughly assess their suitability.

Locate trails so as to utilize existing trailhead facilities (such as parking for a hiking trail); this allows for optimum use and promotes lower costs. Parking facilities, whether existing or planned, should be capable of handling probable use levels in a safe manner. Since winter driving can be hazardous, entrances to parking areas should not be steep, narrow, or have poor visibility. Ability to remove snow easily from parking facilities is also important.

Where feasible, consider using existing trails or roads for hikers, horseback riders, or summer off-road vehicles. Of course, some existing trails or roads may be unusable for ski touring because of bog bridges, waterbars, or drainage dips. Bog bridges, unless there is sufficient snow cover, may stick up through the snow, presenting obstacles to skiers. Waterbars and drainage dips may create rough spots; also, if the water in them does not freeze there may be open, snowless gullies. Hiking trails also may not be sufficiently wide to safely accommodate skiing, particularly on slopes. To widen them sufficiently might detrimentally affect the aesthetics for hikers.

Probably the best formats for ski touring trail layout are single loops, compound or stacked loops or mazes, and variations on them.

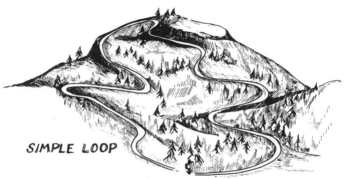

SIMPLE LOOP

Such configurations allow skiers to travel over one or more trail sections, cover variable distances, and return to the same starting point, thus not requiring special transportation arrangements. Where a system of trails is to serve a spectrum of ski touring expertise, a series of loops with various levels of difficulty may work well.

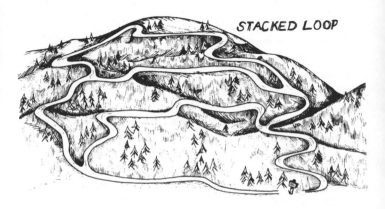

STACKED LOOP

Loops, particularly ones that are used primarily in one direction, also minimize collisions and unexpected meetings between skiers, reduce traffic congestion, and provide skiers with a greater sense of solitude.

Of course, straight line trails between two points are also desirable in some cases, such as in trails connecting two ski touring systems or going from one inn to another. Several ski touring trails exist in the White Mountains — and there are possibly others elsewhere — that leave the top of an alpine ski area and are downhill runs for their entire length to the valley below. Ski tourers purchase a one-way lift ticket to the summit and the beginning of the ski touring trail. In some cases, due to terrain or landowner limitations, it may not be possible to

develop loop trails to and from a natural feature or facility, and thus a straight single trail which must be backtracked has to be used.

## Location Considerations

Sufficient and suitable snow cover is essential to the proper location of any ski touring trail. Climatological data should be reviewed to assess this factor. Orientation of slopes to be crossed, as well as type and quantity of vegetation present, are important factors. South- and west-facing slopes are more exposed to the sun's rays and witness greater melting and evaporation of snow. Sparse vegetation results in poor snow retention, and the wind and sun take their toll on both snow and skier. Northern or easterly slopes should be favored, as well as areas of denser vegetation — the latter particularly if a south or west slope must be traversed, since the snow cover will be shaded from the sun. Dense softwood stands, however, do have the disadvantage that the trees hold much of the snow off the ground. This creates less snow cover upon which to ski. And, since the snow is in the trees and more exposed to the sun, it melts and drops on to the trail, creating more icy conditions than would be found on a trail through a hardwood or mixed stand.

Avoid areas of known avalanche danger, as well as hazardous crossings of lakes, ponds, and streams. Bypass critical wildlife habitats. Strive to avoid or minimize conflicts with other winter recreationists, such as snowmobilers, through separation of the user groups and provision of adequate visual and sound buffers. Crossings of plowed roads, particularly those that are sanded and salted, should be avoided for safety reasons and because skis may be damaged in crossing. Road crossings or trails closely paralleling roads should also be avoided to eliminate vehicle noise and sightings, which may adversely affect the aesthetics of this unmechanized recreational activity. Fence crossings may be difficult, and fences are hazardous when near downhill runs. Thus, they should be avoided.

Avoid boggy or wet areas, since springs and seepage may freeze late and open up early — if they freeze at all — leaving the trail impassable. Stream crossings that must be made should have easy, gentle access if done without a bridge. If a bridge is desired or necessary, stream banks should be high, stable, and as close together as possible to provide for secure bridge bases and to keep span length to a minimum.

It is desirable to have undulating terrain for a varied ski touring experience. Very rough terrain should be avoided, however; such features as boulder fields require greater snow cover depth before they become skiable. The smoother the treadway, the sooner skiing can begin and the longer the season. Long, steep sidehill traverses should be avoided. Skiers may lose edge control and slide downhill when icy conditions exist. And, sidehill traverses result in one ski being lower then the other, forcing weight shifts and an awkward position which can be tiring and difficult to hold. Grooming may be difficult, if not impossible, on steep sidehills. Old logging roads and railroad beds may make good trails. Look also for naturally occurring terraces and benches to provide a smooth run. Avoid rough terrain and steep sidehills.

Routing should be done so as to minimize long, straight stretches of trail, which can be boring; they may also allow skiers to build up undesirable speed. On the other hand, the trail should not be overly sinuous, and sharp corners should be avoided.

## Construction

Many of the techniques and tools used in hiking trail construction, covered elsewhere in this guide, apply to ski touring trails; thus, they will not be discussed here. Instead, trail standards and specialized techniques will be the focus.

**Trail Width** — The width of a ski touring trail depends on the type and amount of use, the slope, and trail layout. Developed, high standard trails which are to be groomed of course require a wide trail to allow for grooming machinery — probably 10-12 feet wide or more. This allows for the setting up of two tracks if desired. A moderate use trail designed to have one set track might be 8-10 feet wide, whereas a low use groomed trail might be 4-6 feet wide. Slope affects width because of the need to snowplow while going downhill or to herringbone to get uphill; sloping trails should be at least 8-10 feet wide on an ungroomed trail. On corners, the trail should be cut wider to allow for turning and snowplowing.

Cut stumps as flush with the ground as possible and trim limbs flush with the tree trunk. Leave no protruding, sharply-pointed stumps or limbs, which could be a hazard to skiers.

**Height** — Branches should be removed to a height of 7-8 feet above the highest level of the snow cover. Evergreen limbs which droop under the weight of snow should be pruned higher.

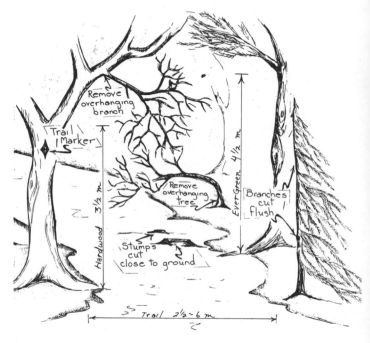

**Trail Tread** — As noted earlier, the smoother the trail tread, the sooner the trail can be skied and the longer the skiing season will last. Therefore, remove large rocks, cut stumps flush, and avoid unreasonably rough terrain and boulder fields.

On some high standard multiple-use ski touring trails, such as those found at the Northfield (Massachusetts) Mountain Recreation Center, extensive tread work is done. The trail base is smoothed and slightly crowned in the middle to allow for drainage, extensive drainage work alongside and underneath the trail is done, and the top is capped with a layer of wood chips. Large machinery is used and cost can be high, but a very durable, low maintenance tread is the result. It can be used in the winter by skiers, with very little snow cover required, and in the summer by hikers, joggers, and horseback riders.

If any sidehill cuts are made and the tread disturbs the ground cover, seeding or mulching should be done to stabilize the soil. Traverses of steep sidehills can be made by sidehill grubbing to create a terrace which will hold snow and provide a level tread. The placement of logs and brush on the downhill side of a sloped traverse can also do the same job by collecting and holding snow to create a terrace. Brush and logs can be placed in depressions and around rocks or high roots to provide fill on which snow will collect, providing a smoother tread. Be sure that brush used for this does not have limbs that will protrude to create a hazard.

Log corduroy, hay, or brush can be used to traverse wet or boggy areas that cannot be avoided. Sometimes ditching can be done to drain an area, but then the ditch may present an obstacle requiring a small bridge. A culvert would eliminate this need.

**Gradient** — Variety and challenge should be objectives for all ski touring trails. Therefore, one should avoid sustained uphill or downhill grades and long, flat sections. Over the length of any given trail a terrain mix of approximately one-third flat, one-third uphill, and one-third downhill is good.

Grades of 7-8% or less are recommended for novice trails. Intermediate trails should have extended grades of no more than 12-15%, while expert trails should have long sections with grades no greater than 20-25%. A 40% grade is generally considered the maximum for even expert skiers. Short sections of higher than average grade are acceptable at all three levels of difficulty.

As mentioned earlier, the steeper the grade, the wider the trail should be to allow skiers to snowplow and herringbone. On corners, widening alone may not be sufficient. Runouts should be provided on corners with steep slopes; this can be done by clearing the outside of the corner from just before where it begins and continuing well past it. The turning radius of corners should increase as slope increases.

Switchbacks may be necessary in some cases to reduce the grade and shorten the length of the downhill run.

Excessive speeds — over 20 miles per hour — should be avoided to minimize loss of control by the skier. Below is a table giving approximate distances the skier will go in attaining such a speed on slopes of varying degrees of steepness. These estimates should prove useful in field inspections, where it may be necessary to gauge permissible grades in combination with length of runout.

| Grade | | Maximum Length in Feet |
|:---:|:---:|:---:|
| In Percent | In Degrees | to Reach 20 MPH |
| 10 | 6 | 250-300 |
| 12 | 7 | 100-125 |
| 15 | 9 | 80 |
| 20 | 12 | 60 |
| 25 | 14 | 40 |
| 30 | 17 | 30 |

From *New York State Department of Environmental Conservation*

**Length** — Novice trails should generally be 3-5 miles in length or less. Intermediate trails — possibly a combination of both easy and more difficult trails — might be 5-8 miles. Expert trails can be longer. Integrated systems of novice, intermediate, and expert trails will provide opportunities for trips of varied length and will accommodate both the afternoon and evening skier, as well as the full-day skier.

**Bridges** — For a complete discussion of bridging techniques for ski touring trails, see Chapter 9 on stream crossings.

## Trail Signing and Marking

The different classifications of ski touring trails, as well as information on distances, should be at all trailheads and junctions or on a map of the area. Some facilities also have a large map of the entire area and all the trails at a main trailhead. Information boards listing trail conditions, wax of the day, and whether or not trails are open or closed are another item found on some trails.

The standard difficulty markers used by most ski touring organizations are shown on page 154. They have been adopted by the U.S. Forest Service, U.S. Ski Association, and National Ski Touring Operators Associations. Printed on heavy plastic, they are quite durable. An exclamation point is often used to mark the beginning of a steep descent or a sharp corner.

Blue plastic diamonds are the standard used to mark most ski trails. All plastic signs and markers can be purchased through the National Ski Touring Operators Association, P.O. Box 557, Brattleboro, Vermont 05301.

Signs and markers should be placed approximately five feet above the highest level of the snow cover. If nailed to trees, use aluminum nails, leaving the heads sticking out about ¼-½ inch to allow for tree growth. If you do not, the tree will grow outward over the nail, causing the sign or marker to pucker up. Aluminum nails will not damage sawmill or pulp mill equipment, should the tree eventually be logged. Treeless areas or areas with extremely deep snow can be marked using poles set in the snow.

## Mapping

Any map for a ski touring trail or system should be easy to read, accurate, and should include references to the difficulty rating of each trail. Trails as well as junctions can be numbered or lettered in the field as well as on the map for easy reference by skiers.

## Facilities

On longer trails consideration may be given to providing warming huts, and possibly overnight accommodations. Also, on long trails into remote or rough areas, first aid caches might be strategically placed.

# 12

# TOOLS: USE, CARE, AND SUPPLIERS

THE PURPOSE OF THIS CHAPTER IS threefold: to generally acquaint the trail maintainer with various types of tools and equipment; to briefly outline their proper use, care, and applicable safety procedures; and, to provide information on sources where such tools can be purchased.

The types of tools used in trail maintenance will vary depending upon the type of work engaged in. One should always have the right tool for the right job.

In addition to describing hand tools, this chapter will discuss some basic power tools. However, information provided on their use is limited; the manufacturers of this equipment can supply a great deal of information that will adequately meet the requirements of anyone interested.

Experience has taught that only top quality tools should be purchased. To make use of ''bargain'' tools will usually only result in headaches for the trail worker.

**Cutting Tools**

Cutting tools are the most important type used in trail work. All trails require clearing of trees and brush during their initial development, as well as annually thereafter.

Cutting tools are the most difficult and elaborate tools in terms of the maintenance they require; in addition, high quality tools may be difficult to procure. Many stores carry simple tools such as axes, saws, and pruners; however, some are often made of poor quality steel and are poorly made, meant only for light use by homeowners.

Tools covered here include axes, saws, pruners, machetes, and specialized tools such as brush or bush hooks and safety axes.

**The Axe** — The axe is undoubtedly one of man's oldest tools. It has played a tremendously important role throughout history. In America it has probably played a more important part than the rifle in the country's development. It was in America that the axe reached its highest form; nowhere else in the world has it been used so much, undergone so many changes, and seen so many adaptations to different uses. Unfortunately, today the axe is diminishing in its importance and popularity. Because of this it is very difficult to find a good axe made with high quality steel.

The axe, however, continues to be an important tool in trail work. On the AMC trail crew it is the primary tool used to cut logs for trail reconstruction. It is also used to remove winter blowdowns.

If used correctly and maintained properly, the axe can be just as effective, efficient, and safe as the crosscut saw or even (in the case of long distance backcountry trail work) the chainsaw. It is lighter than the chainsaw and does not require as many accessories. In addition to being a very practical tool for trail work, it is also a very aesthetic tool which, because of its ancient roots, has great appeal for many trail workers. Aside from replacing the handle every year or so, maintaining an axe is an expense-free proposition, unlike the continued cost of operating a chainsaw.

The two basic kinds of axes are the single bit and the double bit.

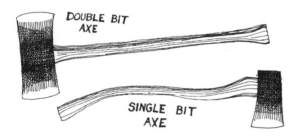

Both can be used for removing blowdowns, limbing, felling trees, cutting notches and waterbars, and topping bridges.
have two blades, one that was kept extremely sharp for felling,
The single bit is the more familiar of the two types. The double bit was more popular in the past, when axemen needed to have two blades, one that was kept extremely sharp for felling, limbing, and notching and the other for chopping close to the ground or in situations which would otherwise dull the good edge. Some feel that the double bit is better balanced, the cutting edge being balanced by the duller edge at the other end of the blade.

For safety reasons a single bit is most popular today. The flat head of the single bit axe can also be helpful for occasionally pounding stakes. However, care should be used in this situation, because the axe head can quite easily be beaten out of shape and the eye become too wide for the wooden handle. It is best to use a sledgehammer for operations which require heavy pounding.

The axe is a very personal tool. The type of axe as well as the style of the head is usually a matter of taste on the part of the axeman; however, the job that the axe is going to be used for is also an important criterion. Single bit axes are the easiest to find, and therefore will probably be the best choice for most people.

The size of the axe is one personal aspect of choosing a good tool. Normally chopping work is done with a three- to 3½-pound axe head. Smaller people may prefer a lighter axe. Big folks might want a four- or even 4½-pound axe; however, they should probably try one out before selecting this larger size. In addition to the weight of the head, the length of the handle is an important consideration. Shorter people want a shorter axe handle (28-30''), whereas taller people want a longer one (32-36''). If the axe is going to be used for clearing small brush and working in cramped quarters, then a smaller handle is more appropriate.

A good quality axe is made of two different kinds of steel. Mild steel, which is softer and therefore more resistant to impact, makes up the eye or the body of the axe. The edge of the axe is made of a harder carbon steel that is forged to the body; it will take and hold a sharp edge. Most axes that are available today are drop-forged and made of one kind of steel. Because of this they may be hard and brittle, making it difficult to maintain a good edge. They may also be somewhat more prone to metal fatigue. Some of these drop-forged axes have broken when they have been used on frozen or hard wood. In shopping for an axe look for a seam and hammer marks between the eye and the edge of the axe; this indicates that it is made of two different kinds of steel. An axe head that is painted or otherwise obscured, especially in the vicinity of the edge, is probably drop-forged. A good place to look for a good quality axe is at an antique store or antique sales. The older axes found in such circumstances are often handmade and of generally higher quality than modern mass-produced axes.

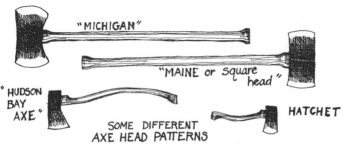

SOME DIFFERENT
AXE HEAD PATTERNS

**Sharpening an Axe** — All cutting tools, including axes, are actually safest when kept sharp. This is because the axe will penetrate the wood rather than deflect in a dangerous glancing blow. Besides being safer, sharp tools are obviously much more efficient to use.

Sharpening an axe well can be tedious; however, it is a fairly straightforward process, requiring only time, practice, and a few simple implements. The most critical aspect of the axe edge is the *bevel*, which is basically the shape of the edge itself.

Bevel A, over, usually develops in an older axe that has been improperly maintained. Sharpening has obviously been con-

USE A LOW SPEED
WHEEL AND KEEP
IT **WET**
ALSO NOTE ANGLE
OF AXE TO
WHEEL

centrated on the edge, which in turn has rounded out the steel into a fairly blunt profile. Bevel B is the proper bevel. The axe is thin enough so that it penetrates deeply into wood but not so thin, as in Bevel C, as to make the edge fragile and prone to breaking. To work a bevel down and get it into shape, as in B below, work the steel down with either a good manual stone on a wheel or a flat bastard file. When using a wheel, always keep its surface wet to carry away any grit that would clog it up, as well as to prevent friction and overheating of the axe head. Water or a light oil is often used on hand stones.

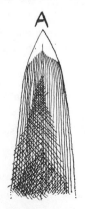
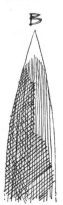
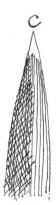

A                   B                   C

Never use an electric grinding wheel to sharpen an axe, as the heat will destroy the temper of the steel. If a hand- or foot-powered wheel is not available, a flat bastard file can be used. Always sharpen into the blade; otherwise, the edge will become a small piece of wire-like metal that will break off with use. By sharpening into the blade, this burr will not form. One should use extreme care when sharpening in this manner, because the hand is proceeding in the direction of the blade. It may be best in this situation to wear a good pair of heavy leather gloves.

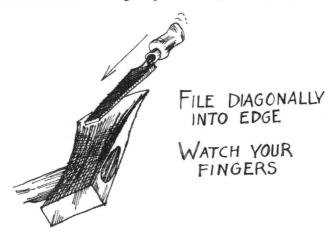

FILE DIAGONALLY
INTO EDGE

WATCH YOUR
FINGERS

Work the bevel down until it looks thin enough to slide easily into wood behind the cutting edge. Once the proper bevel is attained, take a round handstone and hone the edge smooth. If a very keen edge is desired, a finer stone such as an Arkansas handstone can be used. This final part of the process can produce an edge that is fine enough to shave with. Many people achieve an excellent edge with a file. A sharpening stone may be preferable, however, since frequent filing rapidly wears down the blade.

START GRINDING
FROM 3" BACK
AND WORK
TOWARD EDGE

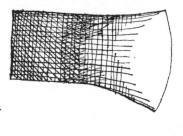

A FAN SHAPE WILL
REINFORCE THE
CORNERS

Again, it should be emphasized that an axe should be kept as sharp as possible at all times. Maintaining a "keen edge" is well worth the effort.

**Rehandling an Axe** — Handles wear out and require eventual replacement. Sometimes they warp or get cracked or broken — or the axe head may loosen, in which case the axe-man will want to replace the handle.

The first step is removal of the old handle. The easiest and fastest way to do this is to saw the handle off the axe head. Then place the head in either a vise or on wooden blocks and drill out the wood in the eye of the axe with an electric or hand-operated drill. By boring out these holes, the pressure of the wood within the axe head is relieved so that the wood can be removed with a hammer and a blunt metal object.

Choose the new handle considering the desired length. When purchasing a new handle look closely at the grain of the wood. It should be fairly straight and close together. If the grain is wide or is not parallel with the axis of the handle, it is probably weak and prone to breaking. Avoid knots at all costs.

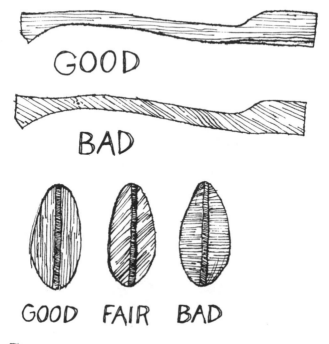

GOOD

BAD

GOOD   FAIR   BAD

PAY CLOSE ATTENTION TO
THE END GRAIN— A TIGHT
GRAIN PARALLEL TO THE
WEDGE IS BEST

Hickory is the best wood for handles because it has a lot of spring and strength. Avoid handles which are painted, since painting covers up any faults in the wood.

The next step involves fitting the handle into the eye. Use a draw shave, wood rasp, or spoke shave to shape the eye down to the size of the head. Remove wood cautiously so that you do not make the handle too thin. Once you can get the head to slide one-third of the distance onto the axe handle, you have probably shaved off enough wood. If the handle head has not been cut down the center at the factory to accept a wooden wedge, you will have to cut a slit yourself. Place the handle in a vise and cut it carefully with a carpenter saw, keeping it centered. Cut it about two-thirds as deep as the eye of the axe head is long.

DRIVE HANDLE INTO
HEAD WITH A
WOODEN OR LEATHER
MALLET

At this point the handle can be held vertically so that the head is down and a hammer is used to pound the end of the handle, drawing the head tightly onto it. Pound the handle in so that it goes past the top of the axe head and comes down to the proper place on the handle. Next the excess wood sticking out of the top of the axe should be cut off and a hardwood wedge driven into the axe head to secure it in place. Using a wooden wedge is better than using a metal one because metal crushes the grain of the wood within the eye of the head; this weakens the handle and makes it prone to loosening. Also, steel wedges are harder to remove when replacing a broken handle.

Another way to secure the head to the handle is to use epoxy and a plastic wedge. The U.S. Forest Service Equipment Development Center in Missoula, Montana greatly reduced loose and broken handles by using epoxy to bond the head to the handle and by epoxying in a plastic wedge. The plastic wedge will not shrink and loosen, and the epoxy further guarantees a tight fit.

To remove a broken handle simply drill out the handle as you would normally and then place the head in boiling water to loosen the epoxy. Special industrial epoxies should not be used, since they require a much higher temperature to loosen.

**Care of the Handle** — There are several improvements the axeman can make on his handle which will make it easier on his hands. Proper care can also eliminate dry rot, loosening, and premature cracking of the handle.

Store bought handles come with either a paint or a hard spar varnish finish which, with extensive use, can cause blistered hands. A finish of boiled linseed oil is best. Apply it with a brush or rag after sanding off the store bought finish.

To extend the life of a handle, linseed oil can be periodically placed in one or two holes drilled in the end of handle; the holes should be about one-quarter inch in diameter and one-half inch deep. At the end of the work day, place several drops of linseed oil in the holes and set the axe handle upright to soak overnight. The natural capillary action of the wood will draw the oil into the grain.

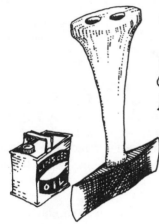

FEED YOUR AXE

PUT LINSEED OIL IN THE HOLES DRILLED IN THE HANDLE — ADDS LIFE!

If a handle loosens within the head of the axe, a temporary solution is to soak the axe head in a bucket of water overnight. This causes the wood to swell and tighten within the head. Mind you, this is a temporary solution. The handle should eventually be replaced. Remember to tape or oil the axe head before immersion.

Do not store an axe for a long period of time by leaning it in a corner. The handle will develop a bend. Hang it up instead.

This is a very cursory overview of taking care of an axe. Patience and persistence will help the axeman gain the skills necessary to care for his tool.

**Axe Sheaths** — All axes should be sheathed to protect both the edge of the axe and people when the axe is being transported or stored. There are many different kinds which can be purchased or made by the axeman. The most common ones on the market are leather sheaths with snaps.

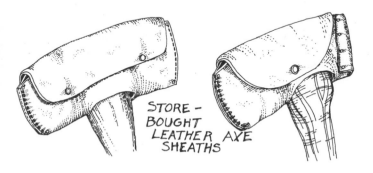

STORE-BOUGHT LEATHER AXE SHEATHS

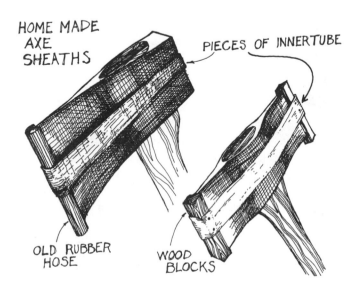

HOME MADE AXE SHEATHS

PIECES OF INNERTUBE

OLD RUBBER HOSE

WOOD BLOCKS

Simple sheaths can be made using rubber from an old garden hose. The hose is cut to the width of the blade and slit along its length. This piece is held against the edge of the axe with a piece of rubber inner tube. This method can also be used with a hollowed out block of wood instead of hose. Wood is obviously more secure and stronger than rubber hose. Wood is also less prone to slipping off the blade. Staple or screw the inner tube to the wood sheath so the separate pieces will not get lost.

**Pulaski** — This tool, with a single bit axe blade and a small grub hoe blade, is used by some. It is good for sidehill grubbing, for removal of blowdowns, and for cleaning drainage during patrolling or other trail maintenance.

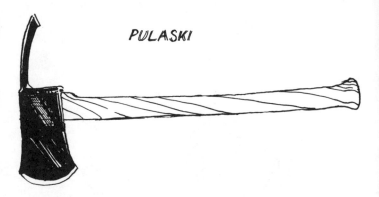

PULASKI

**The Swizzle Stick** — This important and versatile tool was developed for clearing brush and low growth along hiking trails. Similar tools are commercially available; however, they generally lack the strength and durability of the homemade variety. Some have straight edges, others serrated blades.

A swizzle stick is used in a swinging motion similar to a golf club. One with a double-edged blade enables the worker to cut on the backswing as well. The swizzle should always be used firmly, with two hands on the handle to fully control the swing. A rock or stump may accidentally deflect the tool; therefore, always wear heavy boots when using this tool. Also, maintain a good distance between trail workers.

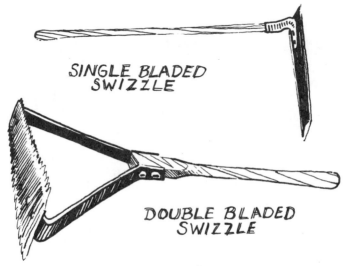

SINGLE BLADED SWIZZLE

DOUBLE BLADED SWIZZLE

A blade sheath should be used when carrying and storing the swizzle. A strip of heavy canvas or old fire hose wrapped around the blade and held in place by inner tube rubber shaped in a figure eight works well. Adhesive tape can be used in a pinch. A wooden or leather sheath can also be made.

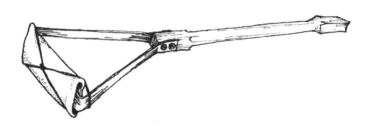

**Sharpening** — A round stone should be used to sharpen the cutting edges. Should the edges get very dull or battered from use, a flat mill bastard file is a helpful preliminary to the stone. Sharpen only on the low side of the blade; otherwise, sharpening is similar to that used on the axe.

SHARPENING A SWIZZLE

FOLLOW
THIS BEVEL

FILE INTO
EDGE

WATCH YOUR
FINGERS!

**Construction of the Swizzle Stick** — Construction of a homemade swizzle is quite simple. A hardwood handle is used, with ash or hickory preferred. Someone with a wood lathe should have no problem making one. In a pinch a sledgehammer handle will do. The steel frame can be easily bent using a torch or forge. The blade is the most difficult part, requiring the help of a machinist or blacksmith to get the proper temper to hold a good cutting edge. The edge should not be too hard or it will break upon striking a rock or root, but it cannot be too soft either or it will not hold an edge.

In putting the swizzle together the bolts holding the blade to the frame should be heat treated for strength. Flat washers are necessary in order to dissipate vibrations from impact. Without them the blade will soon begin to fatigue and crack. When using the tool in the field it is a good idea to carry spare bolts, nuts, washers, and wrenches. To minimize loosening and loss of bolts and nuts, the end of the bolt can be hammered or filed, or the commercial compound Locktite can be used. The bolt can also be drilled with a hole and a cotter pin inserted.

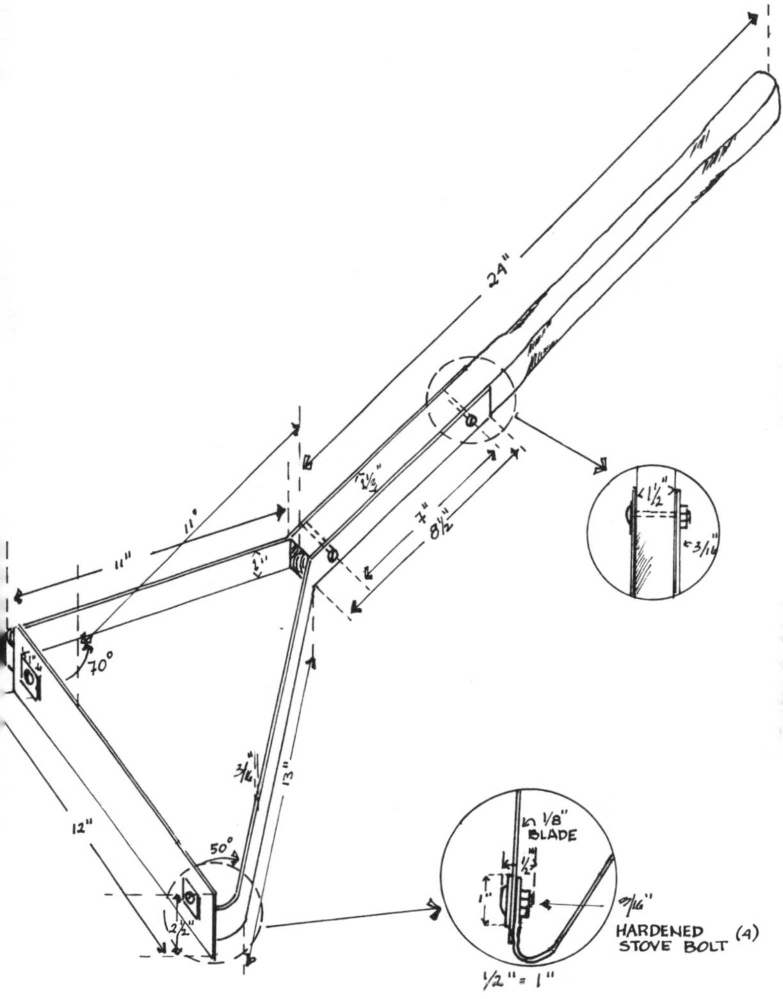

24"

2⅓"

11"

11"

7"

8½"

1"

70°

1½"

←3/16

3/16"

13"

12"

50°

2½"

⅛"
BLADE

3/16"

HARDENED
STOVE BOLT (4)

½" = 1"

*Plan for swizzle*

Customizing a swizzle stick involves lengthening or shortening the handle. Some maintainers wrap black electrician's tape around the handle, sometimes with a thin piece of foam or ensolite, to cushion the handle slightly. A large knot on the end, either shaped from the wood or from wrapping it with tape, helps keep the hands from slipping off.

The frame can also be changed, shortening or lengthening one side or the other, to get a sharper angle. Some prefer to have the blade horizontal to the ground when holding the tool out at the angle they are most comfortable with.

**Safety Axe, Brush Hook, and Machete** — These can be handy supplements to the more classic tools used for trail clearing. They require care and sharpening similar to that described for the axe.

The safety axe is a good tool for younger, less experienced trail workers, because the blade is less exposed than that of an axe or machete. If the blade is damaged, it can be replaced. It is particularly effective on young, springy hardwood growth.

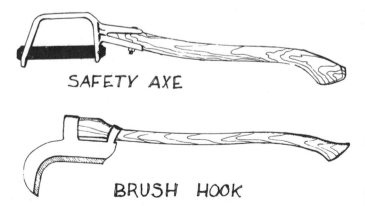

SAFETY AXE

BRUSH HOOK

The bush or brush hook is another type of tool available for clearing brush.

The best machete for trail clearing is probably the Woodsmen's Pal. It has some features, such as a cutting hook, which are unavailable on a conventional machete. It is also shorter than the conventional tool, which allows a shorter, more controlled swing.

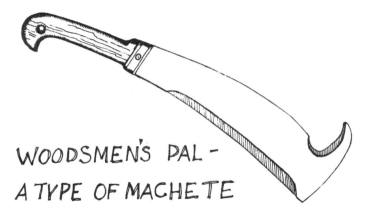

WOODSMEN'S PAL –
A TYPE OF MACHETE

As with the swizzle stick, all of these tools should be used with care. A good grip at all times, plenty of space between workers, and a little looking and thought before swinging will prevent accidents and damage to the tools.

With the Woodsmen's Pal in particular, if the hook is used in pruning limbs or cutting or uprooting undergrowth, caution must be exercised. Many people grab the limb or bush with one hand to toss it away once it is cut. They hook it at the base and pull toward them. If the hook slips it may catch the fingers of the other hand. In swinging the Woodsmen's Pal be careful not to bring it too near your head. You might catch your shirt collar, ear, or the side of your head with the hook.

The sharpening of all these tools can be done with a round stone and flat bastard file. All should have store-bought or homemade sheaths, as outlined for the axe.

Most trail workers seem to prefer hand saws or clippers for limbing and other brushing, as they leave a cleaner, smoother cut and are safer to use. These other tools often leave a sharply pointed stub.

**Lopping Shears, Pole Clippers, and Hand Pruners** — Long-handled clippers, pruners, or lopping shears come in a variety of styles. Handles are made of wood, steel, or aluminum. Cutting heads are either the sliding-blade-and-hook type or the anvil type. Some have simple pivot actions, while others have compound or gear-driven actions for increased cutting power. Most cut up to between one- and 1¾-inch limbs.

For specialized work such as clearing ski touring trails, a variety of pole clippers are manufactured for professional tree trimming work. These are suitable for clipping high limbs up to one or 1½ inches in diameter. Generally a six- to eight-foot handle is sufficient for ski touring trail work. Longer handles can be obtained.

Small hand pruners can sometimes be quite handy for occasional light pruning. These also come in a wide variety of styles.

Since clippers or lopping shears are one of the primary tools of the trail maintainer, it is important that high quality ones be obtained. Look for brand name shears that are built for rugged use and that are simple to maintain and repair. Some of the

# DIFFERENT TYPES OF PRUNERS

## SLIDING BLADE TYPE WOODEN HANDLES

## ANVIL TYPE w/ COMPOUND GEAR w/ WOODEN HANDLES

## SLIDING BLADE w/ COMPOUND GEAR DRIVEN TYPE

## ANVIL BLADE RACHET TYPE

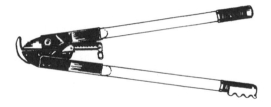

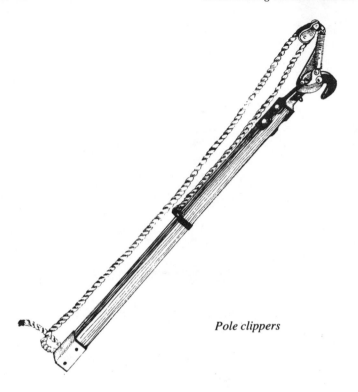

*Pole clippers*

cheaper models available have handles that are simply glued or riveted on loosely. The blades are made of steel that is too soft. Some can be bent by cutting small hardwood bushes or limbs. Also, some poorly made clippers of the sliding blade type have flimsy handles or stops that do not meet correctly. When pressure is applied and the stops slip by each other, the handles come together and pinched fingers result. Head assemblies and gear mechanisms should be tight, not loose with lots of play in them.

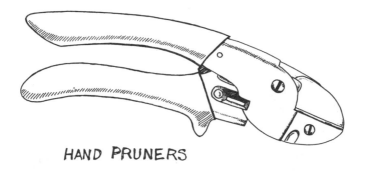

HAND PRUNERS

Clippers that are ruggedly built for heavy duty cutting, though they tend to be a bit on the heavy side, will be best in the long run. Gear-driven clippers with the anvil-type blade have worked best for the AMC to date. All parts are easily replaceable, should anything break. Ask local tree companies or landscapers what tools work best for them.

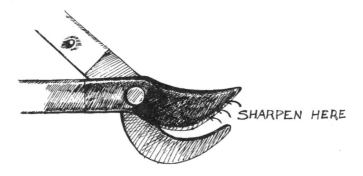

SHARPEN HERE

Clippers should be kept sharp and all metal parts lightly oiled. A flat file or handstone works well for sharpening the blade. With the sliding blade type of pruners, only the outside edge of the cutting blade should be sharpened.

By concentrating sharpening on the curved outside edge of the cutting blade with scissor-type clippers, the jaws of the pruner are forced together during the cut. Sharpening the inside edge of the blade will form a bevel that will tend to force the jaws apart during the cut. The anvil-type pruners are sharpened on both sides of the cutting blade. Care must be taken to sharpen such blades evenly along their length and at the proper bevel.

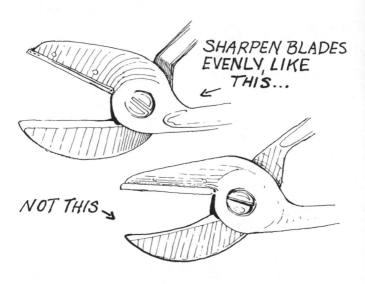

SHARPEN BLADES
EVENLY, LIKE
THIS...

NOT THIS

**Crosscut Saws** — There are two types of crosscut saws.[1] The one-man crosscut, three to 4½ feet in length, is designed to be used by one man on small timber; however, it can be converted into a two-man saw if desired by attaching a supplementary handle at the end of the blade. The two-man crosscut,

---

[1] Most of the information on crosscut saws was developed using *Crosscut Saw Manual* by Warren Miller, U. S. Department of Agriculture, Forest Service, Equipment and Development Center, Missoula, Montana, June, 1977.

generally five to eight feet in length, is designed for cutting larger diameter timber.

*1 MAN CROSSCUT SAW WITH HANDLE FOR 2-MAN OPTION*

*2-MAN CROSSCUT SAW*

Three common tooth patterns are available, each designed for a specific type of wood. The perforated lance tooth style is best for cutting softwoods. The champion tooth style is for cutting hardwoods or frozen timber. The plain tooth style is designed for cutting dead, dry wood.

*PERFORATED LANCE TOOTH*

CHAMPION TOOTH

PLAIN TOOTH

The cutting teeth sever the fibers on each side of the cut. The raker teeth, cutting like a plane bit, peel the cut fibers and collect them in the gullets between the cutting teeth and raker teeth and carry them out of the cut. A properly sharpened crosscut saw cuts deep and makes thick shavings.

As few people know how to properly maintain a crosscut saw, they are not often used today. The axe, chainsaw, and bow saw are more commonly used. As is the case with the axe, the crosscut has become for the most part a tool of the past because of the development of the chainsaw.

Crosscuts do, however, have some advantages over the axe and even the chainsaw which may make them a good choice for large cutting projects. They are inexpensive, lightweight, non-polluting in terms of noise and fumes, safer than the axe, and

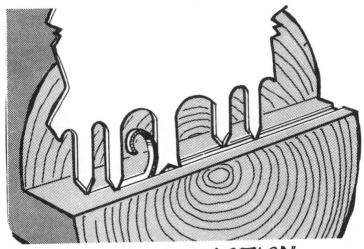

## CUTTING ACTION
## OF CROSSCUT SAW

relatively easy to use. They can be just as efficient and effective as the chainsaw, especially when the tool must be carried long distances. Sometimes, however, finding someone who can sharpen a crosscut properly can be a problem. If this proves to be the case, small, relatively inexpensive sharpening kits can be obtained, as well as excellent instructions for doing your own crosscut maintenance.

As for use and safety tips, a few things should be kept in mind. When felling timber you should use the same basic technique as outlined for felling with a chainsaw or axe. To keep your crosscut from binding, carry a small container of kerosene and lightly coat the blade with it. For transporting a crosscut, the best sheath is one made of two strips of plywood held together over the blade with three or four bolts.

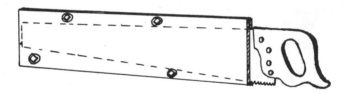

## PLYWOOD SAW SHEATH

**Bow Saws and Pruning Saws** — Bow saws, sometimes known as pulpwood saws, and the smaller pruning saws come in a wide variety of sizes and shapes. The choice of saw depends on the type and amount of work to be done. Some of the larger, older bow saws have wooden frames. Today most such tools have painted or chrome-plated steel or aluminum frames and blades ranging in length from 24 to 36 inches.

The larger bow saws are sometimes used for cutting small diameter timber and for removing blowdowns.

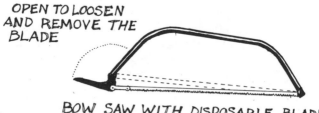

OPEN TO LOOSEN AND REMOVE THE BLADE

BOW SAW WITH DISPOSABLE BLADE AND CLAMP-TYPE HANDLE

The smaller pruning or utility saws are good for sawing small diameter timber such as stakes for log steps and waterbars. They are also good when clearing trail where saplings or limbs are too large for clippers and it is undesirable to leave a pointed stump, as sometimes happens when using an axe or brush hook. There are some collapsible saws on the market which are handy for the occasional user; however, they are generally too lightweight for continuous, heavy-duty use.

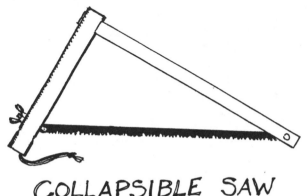

## COLLAPSIBLE SAW FOR BACKPACKING

## A GOOD SMALL PRUNING SAW

For specialized work there are various manufacturers of professional tree trimming equipment who have hand pruning saws. Some have teflon-coated blades for ease of action. There are also various types of pole saws which can be used for cutting high limbs when clearing ski touring trails. Both of these types of saws have teeth that cut on the pull stroke only.

Use and care of these saws is quite similar. Almost all of the bow saws and pruning saws have blades which are replaced rather than sharpened, whereas the professional pruning saws and pole saws can be sharpened. Usually sharpening specialists can be found on a local basis.

When using these saws, be sure that all moving parts such as nuts and bolts are secure, with the blade at the right tension if it is adjustable. If it is too loose or too tight you will end up with a broken blade when it flexes or gets pinched in the wood. Trail experience points toward preference for those saws with the smallest number of movable or adjustable parts (such as wing nuts), which may get lost. It is also wise to bring spare blades and parts when working in the field so that minor repairs can be made.

When transporting or storing saws, some type of sheath should be used to protect the worker as well as the blade. Wood, leather, or heavy canvas can be used. Many bow saws come with hard plastic sheaths. All unpainted metal parts should be kept lightly oiled to prevent rust when not in use.

## Digging Tools

Virtually all trail reconstruction activities require that workers move soil to build steps, waterbars, drainage ditches,

POLE SAW

bridges, and similar projects. Digging tools for accomplishing these tasks are the shovel, mattock, pick, and crowbar.

These tools are very common and no instructions on their use need be given here. There are several types of each, however, that serve specific purposes.

**Shovel** — This tool comes in two forms, the long handle and the "D" handle.

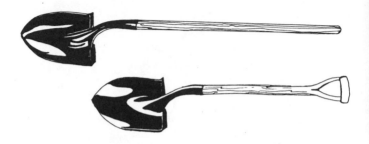

The "D" handle shovel, being shorter, is more appropriate in congested situations. Some also find lifting with this type of shovel to be easier, since the load is closer to the body. Others favor the long-handled shovel, since it offers a longer reach and in some instances requires less bending. Care should be used not to pry too heavily with the shovel; otherwise, the handle will break. A mattock or crowbar should be used if large rocks impede digging. Some maintainers slightly sharpen the shovel's edge to facilitate cutting roots. The AMC trail crew has found it easier to replace broken handles on hollow back shovels than it is for those with a solid shank. You simply grind off the head of the rivet holding the handle to the shank, drive it out, and then drive out the handle. The new handle can be secured with a rivet, a bolt through the shank, or screws through each side.

**Mattock** — In the White Mountains the mattock has become the most important digging tool because of the large numbers of rocks in the mountain soils there. The mattock is a heavy tool that is not easily broken. When used vigorously to dig through roots and to pry and sometimes break rock, surprising amounts of work can be done.

There are two types of mattocks available, both of which have an adze, or a blade set at right angles to the handle for grubbing; they differ by having either a pick or a cutter blade at the other end.

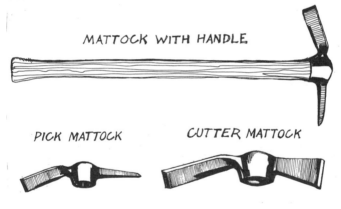

MATTOCK WITH HANDLE

PICK MATTOCK        CUTTER MATTOCK

The pick mattock is more popular with AMC crews because it is much more effective for prying rock. The cutter mattock may be more effective in areas with deeper soils and more roots than rocks.

Care consists of periodic slight sharpening in order to maintain a rudimentary edge capable of effective digging and root cutting. An electric grinding wheel, carefully used, reduces labor time when sharpening. Handles need periodic replacement, so an adequate stock should be kept on hand. Hickory or ash is best.

To keep handles from working loose prematurely you can place a thick, short (¾''– 1'') wood screw, sheet metal screw, or lag bolt into the handle near the mattock head. Prior drilling is advised. Do not place it in the side of the handle, as this is apt to split the wood. This applies to grub and adze hoes also.

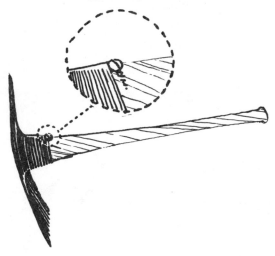

**Grub Hoes, Adze Hoes, and Fire Rakes** — Hoes of various weights are also available and can be used in trail construction and maintenance. Grub hoes are essentially mattocks without a cutter blade or pick. Hoe width is generally 3-4 inches. A standard mattock handle is used.

An adze hoe or hazel hoe is lighter and has a wider blade (5-8 inches), sharper edge, and curved handle. Where lots of sidehill

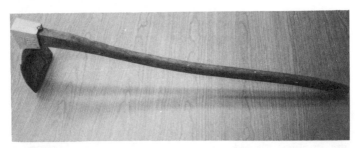

*Adze Hoe*

grubbing has to be done — except where soils are very rocky —
the AMC has found this tool to be the most useful. The wider
blade moves more soil, the sharper edge cuts roots well, and the
curved handle facilitates use. For cleaning waterbars, where it is
desirable to bring the soil up over the waterbar and deposit it on
the downhill side for backfill, and for cleaning drainage ditches,
the adze hoe also works well.

Some trail maintainers use fire rakes for sidehill grubbing and
other tasks quite successfully.

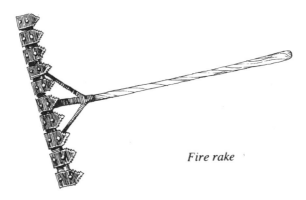

*Fire rake*

**Pick** — A pick is rarely necessary in trail work, its function being adequately served by the pick mattock. However, in jobs which involve a lot of rock work, picks may be appropriate.

**Crowbar** — This tool is an essential one for moving large rocks. With practice the crowbar can become surprisingly effective as a lever for moving great weight. The trick is to place a fulcrum with care and forethought. In order to be most effective the crowbar should have a wedge-shaped tip. Sixteen- to eighteen-pound crowbars are most commonly used. Lighter ones are apt to bend. Heavier ones are rarely necessary.

A bent crowbar can be straightened out by heating it with an acetylene torch or in a forge. Once bent, however, it is likely to become so again as the steel has lost temper.

One AMC crew member developed an attachment for a crowbar which allows it to be used like a peavy or cant-dog. It can be used for rolling logs or moving and twisting the base of a tree being felled when it has gotten hung up in another tree and must be knocked loose. The latter procedure, of course, should be done with the utmost of care.

A digging bar is used for loosening compacted or rocky soil. It has a small blade at one end. Some moving of rock can also be done using these bars, although they are not quite as rugged as the crowbar.

## Measuring Tools

Various tools for measuring distances may be required during layout, reconstruction, and maintenance of trails. Levels, transits, and a theodolite may be necessary in unusually fine map work in laying out a trail or campsite; however, if this degree of accuracy is needed, it is probably best achieved by hiring professionals.

Measuring wheels are used to measure trail distances for guidebook descriptions. They can also be used for marking off an index system for record keeping and work assignments for crews. The AMC has had the best luck with an inexpensive, rugged, all-steel measuring wheel with an internal cable and counter mechanism on the handle. Those with external counters, which sometimes get caught on brush, or bicycle-like wheels, which can get bent easily, have not worked as well. Some enterprising maintainers have made their own measuring tools using a bicycle mileage meter and wheel.

## Power Tools

Though the bulk of trail work involves the use of hand tools, there are occasions where concentrations of heavy cutting or specialized work make power tools more efficient. Information on the chainsaw, motorized brush cutter, and jackhammer is included here. Because manufacturers have much good information on the use and care of these implements, only a broad description of each tool and its specifications is given here.

**Chainsaws** — The chainsaw comes in an extensive variety of makes, sizes, and types, each of which is suited to a particular job. Each of the major manufacturers of chainsaws carries a full line of equipment that graduates in size and power from small six- to eight-pound saws to the large machines used by the pulp and paper industry.

Choosing a make and manufacturer is a matter of personal choice, like choosing an automobile, and the range of opinions among users is as great as the selection itself. The choice of make might most appropriately be determined by investigating what dealerships are available in the purchaser's area. Having a good dealer who provides prompt and efficient service is probably more important than the characteristics of the saws themselves, particularly if the final choice is between any of the large manufacturers that specialize in chainsaws. Chainsaws sold by the large department store outlets are best avoided.

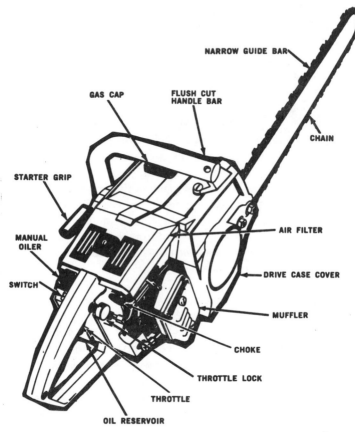

A drawing of a typical chain saw with the various exterior parts labeled.[2]

---

[2]Drawing from Bromley, W.S., *Pulpwood Production,* Interstate Printers and Publishers, Inc., Danville, Illinois, 1969, p. 122. The text following relies heavily on the same source.

The smaller saws available from each of the major manufacturers are naturally the most popular saws for trail work because of their light weight. Larger, more powerful saws are more appropriate for particularly heavy cutting, such as would be the case with major storm damage or when it is necessary to clean up a trail damaged by timber harvesting. These situations are fairly rare for most maintainers, however.

Features to look for in shopping for a saw, after one has decided on an appropriate size, include the general "feel" and appearance of the saw and the accessibility of controls and components — particularly the spark plug, which needs periodic replacement, and the gas and oil filler caps which, if on the same side of the saw, eliminate the need to rotate the unit during fill-ups. All saws should have a throttle-lock which allows the operator to free his hand from the throttle in order to start the saw safely with both hands — one hand to hold the saw on the ground and one to pull the cord.

Most modern saws have a safety feature on the handle which prevents the engine from revving up unless the operator has a firm grip on the saw. Another feature to look for is whether hand grips are rubber mounted to reduce the effect of tiring vibration on the hands. The effectiveness as well as the position of the muffler should also receive consideration. The newer saws are suprisingly quiet and if the muffler is on the front of the saw or on its right side directed away from the operator, then noise and exhaust fumes are less of a problem. The chain needs to be oiled as it rotates on the guidebar; therefore, saws are equipped with either manual or automatic oilers. The automatic is preferable if it is dependable, because while the operator is concentrating on a cut he may neglect to oil his chain, which increases bar and chain wear.

This cursory overview is provided to help people select and purchase saws. The manufacturers supply extensive information which the discreet shopper will do well to read. The opinions of friends and fellow maintainers are also an obvious — and dependable — source of good information on the comparative value of different saws. It may also be beneficial to talk to either a professional tree trimming outfit or a logging operator working in the purchaser's local area. The types of saws they use and their recommendations on dealerships may be helpful.

**Safe Chainsaw Operation** — Safe chainsaw operating techniques should be constantly stressed to all power tool users. The chain operates at a fast cutting speed and the slightest slip or miscalculation can bring extremely serious injury.

There are protective devices available for chainsaw operators and they should be used. They include helmets, eye protection, and, for particularly loud saws used on a long-term basis, ear protection. Additionally, leather gloves should be worn, as well as heavy leather boots with non-slip soles, preferably equipped with steel toe shields. Well fitting, long-sleeved shirts and long pants are warranted.

## CHECK LIST
## FOR THE SAFE AND EFFICIENT OPERATION
## OF YOUR CHAINSAW

☐ READ YOUR OWNER'S MANUAL AND ALL SUPPLEMENTS (if any are enclosed) thoroughly before operating your saw.

☐ DON'T USE ANY OTHER FUEL than that recommended in your Owner's Manual.

☐  REFUEL IN A SAFE PLACE. Don't spill fuel or start saw where you fuel it. Do not refuel a hot saw; allow it to cool off. Be certain the saw has dried thoroughly before starting if fuel has spilled on the unit.

☐  DON'T SMOKE while fueling or operating the saw.

☐  START YOUR SAW WITHOUT HELP. Don't start a saw on your leg or knee. Never operate a chainsaw when you are fatigued.

☐  KEEP ALL PARTS of your body and clothing away from the saw chain when starting or running the engine. Before you start the engine, make sure the saw chain is not contacting anything.

☐  BEWARE OF KICKBACK! Hold saw firmly with both hands when engine is running; use a firm grip with thumbs and fingers encircling the chainsaw handles and watch carefully what you cut. Kickback (saw jumps or jerks up or backward) can be caused by —

RIGHT -fingers wrapped, thumb underneath

WRONG -hand may slip with thumb on top

— Striking limbs or other objects accidentally with the tip of the saw while the chain is moving.

— Striking metal, cement, or other hard material near the wood, or buried in the wood.

— Running engine slowly at start of or during cut.

— Dull or loose chain.

— Cutting above shoulder height.

— Inattention in holding or guiding saw while cutting.

☐ IT IS STRONGLY RECOMMENDED that you do not attempt to operate the saw while IN A TREE, ON A LADDER, or ON ANY OTHER UNSTABLE SURFACE. If you elect to do so, be advised that these positions are EXTREMELY DANGEROUS.

☐ BE SURE OF YOUR FOOTING and pre-plan a safe exit from a falling tree or limbs.

☐ WHEN CUTTING A LIMB THAT IS UNDER TENSION be alert for springback so that you will not be struck when the tension is released.

☐ USE EXTREME CAUTION when cutting small size brush and saplings because slender material may catch the saw chain and be whipped toward you or pull you off balance.

☐ VIBRATION — Avoid prolonged operation of your chainsaw and rest periodically, especially if your hand or arm starts to have a loss of feeling, swells, or becomes difficult to move.

☐ EXHAUST FUMES — Do not operate your chainsaw in confined or poorly ventilated areas.

☐ OBSERVE ALL LOCAL FIRE PREVENTION REGU-LATIONS — It is recommended that you keep a fire ex-tinguisher and shovel close at hand whenever you cut in areas where dry grass, leaves, or other flammable materials are present.

NOTE:  Spark arrester screens are available for installation in your muffler where fire regulations require them. Check local regulations for special requirements.

☐  TURN OFF YOUR SAW WHEN MOVING BETWEEN CUTS and before setting it down. Always carry the chainsaw with the engine stopped, the guide bar and saw chain in the rear, and the muffler away from your body.

☐  USE WEDGES TO HELP CONTROL FELLING and prevent binding the bar and chain in the cut.

☐  DON'T TOUCH or try to stop a moving chain with your hand.

☐  KEEP THE CHAIN SHARP and snug on the guide bar.

☐  DON'T ALLOW DIRT, FUEL, OR SAWDUST to build up on the engine or outside of the saw.

☐  KEEP ALL SCREWS AND FASTENERS TIGHT. Never operate a chainsaw that is damaged, improperly adjusted, or not completely and securely assembled. Be sure that the saw chain stops moving when the throttle control trigger is released. Keep the handles dry, clean, and free of oil or fuel mixture.

**Jackhammers** — The various applications of the self-contained, gas-powered jackhammers were discussed earlier (pages 71-72); therefore, only technical features will be outlined here.

These tools are powered by a single cylinder, two-cycle engine which provides power for three basic operations:

(1) movement of an impact piston which provides the impact on the drill bit, (2) rotation of the drill bit, and (3) compression of gas and transmission through the drill bit, which blows dust out of the hole.

These self-contained units can be packed into remote locations by two crew members, one of whom carries fuel and all accessories. Such units are considerably more limited in their power and applications than is a conventional jackhammer, which is operated by a large and powerful compressor on a trailer or the back of a truck; however, they do enable maintainers with trail problems involving rock to solve them.

There are two manufacturers, both in Sweden. Literature on the features of their equipment will be provided to persons making inquiries.

| Pionjar Distributors | Cobra Distributors |
|---|---|
| Abema, Inc. | Atlas Copco. |
| 129 Glover Ave. | 70 Demarest Dr. |
| P.O. Box 775 | P.O. Box 312 |
| Norwalk, CT 06856 | Wayne, NJ 07470 |

Drill bits, shims, and wedges can be purchased from Bicknell Manufacturing Company, Rockland, Maine.

**Gas-Powered Brush Cutters** — These power tools can be beneficial for trail clearing through young, heavy growth such as can be found after an area has grown back following logging. Few maintainers will have a need to invest in this specialized piece of equipment. It is acknowledged here to let readers know that the tool exists and can be used for certain trail situations. If one is used, the operator should be experienced and careful, working a safe distance from others.

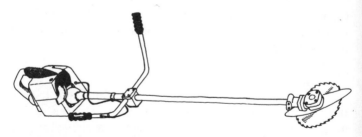

*Gas-powered brush cutter*

**Gas-Powered Winch** — This may have some of the same kinds of applications for various trail maintenance tasks as the hand-operated winch. Securely anchored and utilizing a chainsaw for power, it can be used to move rock and logs.

## Other Tools

Bark spuds or peelers can greatly facilitate peeling logs for trail construction. Before the modern, automated de-barkers used at sawmills and paper mills were invented, all bark removal was done by hand using these simple but effective tools.

*Bark spud*

Come-alongs or cable jacks are sometimes needed for moving large rocks or logs. Most are available with varying pull capacities, anywhere from one ton to three or four tons. Most utilize cable on a spool and can be used as a single or double cable. Some operate with chain. One available model uses internal gears through which a piece of cable of any desired length can be threaded. Cable, chain, or tire chains can be used to wrap a rock for moving it.

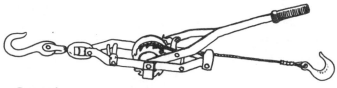

*Come-along*

Splitting wedges or woodchopper's wedges, most commonly used to split firewood, are also used to split logs for split log bog bridges. Weights and sizes vary, but generally a four- to five-pound one, eight to ten inches long and 2½ to three inches wide, is best.

*Splitting wedge*

Timber carriers can sometimes be used to carry large logs for waterbars, bog bridges, and stream bridges, as well as for shelter construction.

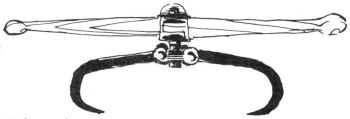

*Timber carrier*

**Packboard** — The Appalachian Mountain Club has developed a packboard to use in resupplying its hut system, and for use by trail crews going out into the field for a week at a time. It is much more rugged and heavy duty than any frames available on the market. Its main purpose is for carrying heavy loads (80-120 pounds) over relatively short distances (3-5 miles). It is included here for those maintainers planning heavy-duty reconstruction work.

The frame is made primarily out of straight-grained white ash, a strong and resilient wood that can withstand the stresses and strains of heavy loads.

The following is a listing of the other materials needed, along with where they can be purchased.

1.  Page Belting Company, 26 Commercial St., Concord, NH 03301 (603-225-5523):
    a) Oak leather pieces for tote harness — 26" long x 2½" wide, 9-10/64" thick, oil dressed.
    b) 1" copper rivets with burrs, 6-10 gauge (sub 7/8").
2.  Any hardware store:
    a) No. 414 nickel buckle with imitation roller, 1¼"— manufactured by Covert Manufacturing Company, Troy, NY.
    b) No. 514 ¼" x 2½" Alt No. 4R2 eye bolt and nut — manufactured by Hindley Manufacturing Company.
3.  Fortune Canvas, 190 US Rt. 1, Falmouth, ME 04105 (207-781-2628):
    a) pack corset.

The approximate cost of all material should run around $50.00.

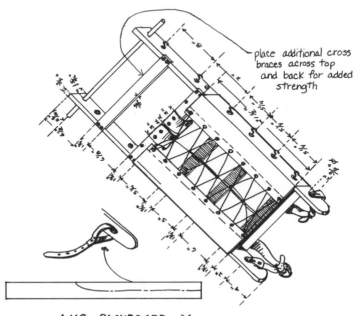

place additional cross
braces across top
and back for added
strength

## AMC PACKBOARD #1
SCALE : ⅛" = 1"    NEW JAN 1977

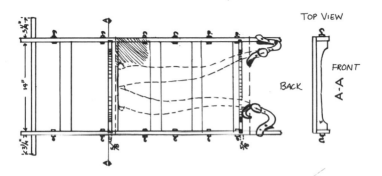

TOP VIEW

FRONT

BACK

A-A

## Safety Equipment

Besides the various sheaths used to protect blades and users, there is a variety of safety equipment available.

Hardhats come in many styles, colors, and materials. Strong, good quality, and comfortable hats should be selected. Color, though seemingly insignificant, can make a difference, in that white or aluminum-colored ones are much cooler than dark ones on hot summer days.

Steel-toed boots are recommended for chainsaw work. Also available are chaps or leggings and chest pads made of very strong but lightweight mesh, much like a bulletproof vest, to give the chainsaw user some margin of protection from cuts.

Safety goggles or face masks are appropriate in chainsaw work and when using a brush cutter or jackhammer. Hearing protectors are also available and should be used when operating motorized tools for ear protection.

Shin guards used by baseball catchers are sometimes used by maintainers engaged in extensive axe work and digging with mattocks. Leather work gloves are preferred by some to protect hands from blistering and cuts.

## SUPPLIERS OF TOOLS, EQUIPMENT, AND MATERIALS FOR TRAIL WORK

In order to facilitate the maintainer's ability to find tools for trail work, the following list of suppliers has been compiled. This list is not complete; it will, however, enable the trail worker to search out the major suppliers meeting his equipment needs. Many of the more common tools, of course, can be purchased from hardware stores, department stores, and the like. The suppliers listed as wholesale will send you a catalog and refer you to dealers in your area. They will not sell directly to you.[3]

## TABLE 1

Tool      Numbers correspond to companies listed in Table 2

Adze Hoe, Hazel Hoe    23, 41, 54
Anti-theft Sign Bolts    60, 65
Axe, Hatchet    3, 4, 5, 14, 21, 23, 24, 30, 37, 55, 58, 59, 61, 62, 69, 74
Bark Spud    55, 62, 69, 74
Boundary Marking Paints and Links    1, 23, 24, 41, 42, 56, 62
Bow Saw    3, 5, 9, 18, 23, 24, 30, 41, 46, 53, 58, 62, 72, 73, 74
Brush Cutters    17, 20, 23, 26, 41, 49, 59, 71, 72, 73
Brush Hook, Bush Hook    3, 5, 19, 23, 24, 27, 41, 54, 61, 62
Chainsaw    7, 20, 23, 26, 28, 31, 40, 41, 71, 72, 73
Clippers, Pruner, Lopping Shears    2, 3, 5, 10, 14, 15, 23, 24, 25, 41, 47, 53, 54, 62, 66
Come Along, Winch    8, 23, 24, 36, 41, 50, 62, 70, 72, 73
Crosscut Saw, Handle    5, 23, 24, 29, 41, 46, 58, 62, 69, 74
Crosscut Saw Sharpening Kit    13, 74
Crowbar, Mattock, Pick, Hoe    9, 34, 41, 54, 63, 67, 68
Fire Rake    19, 23, 41
Flagging Tape    23, 24, 41, 62
Grub Hoe    41, 54, 67, 68
Handles for Axe, Sledge, Mattock    9, 11, 24, 35, 43, 45, 52, 55, 62, 64

---

[3] A portion of this material was developed using tool listings supplied by the U.S. Forest Service, Equipment Development Center, Missoula, Montana 59801.

Layout Equipment (Compass, Inclinometer)   23, 24, 41, 62
Machete, Woodsmen's Pal   5, 14, 15, 23, 24, 41, 44, 62
Measuring Wheel   12, 23, 24, 41, 48, 62
Pole Pruner, Pole Saw   2, 3, 5, 6, 18, 22, 23, 24, 39, 41, 47, 53, 62
Pruning Saw   3, 5, 6, 16, 18, 22, 23, 24, 39, 41, 46, 53, 54, 61, 62
Pulaski   5, 14, 23, 24, 41, 55, 62
Router, Bits, Stencils   32, 38, 51, 57, 58, 69, 72, 73
Safety Equipment   6, 23, 24, 41, 50, 62, 71
Sandstone Grinding Wheel, Sharpening Stones   69 74
Sheath   6, 9, 23, 29, 41, 55, 62
Splitting Wedge   5, 23, 23, 37, 41, 55, 62, 67, 68
Swedish Brush Axe   5, 23, 24, 41, 62
Swizzle, Weeder, Scythe   3, 15, 19, 27, 41, 54, 62, 63
Tamping Bar   24, 34, 61, 62, 63, 67, 68
Timber Carrier, Peavy   5, 23, 33, 41

## TABLE 2

1.  American Coding & Marking Ink , 1220 North Ave., Plainfield, NJ 07062
2.  American Standard Co., 1 West St., Plantsville, CT 06479
3.  Ames, Div. of McDonough Co., PO Box 1774, Parkersburg, WV 26101 (W)
4.  Army Surplus Stores, most cities
5.  Bartlett Mfg. Co., 3003 East Grand Blvd., Detroit, MI 48202
6.  W. M. Bashlin Co., Grove City, PA 16127
7.  Beaird-Poulan Div., Emerson Electric Co., 5020 Flournay/Lucas Rd., Shreveport, LA 71109 (W)

8. Beebe Brothers, Inc., 2724 6th Ave. South, PO Box 3643, Seattle, WA 98124 (W)

9. Belknap, Inc., "Bluegrass," PO Box 28, Louisville, KY 40201 (W)

10. Brookstone Co., "Hard to Find Tools," Peterborough, NH 03458

11. Burroughs-Ross-Colville Co., 301 Depot St., McMinnville, TN 37110

12. Cedarholm Mfg. Co., Bastrop, TX 78602

13. Century Tool Co., Inc., Ginko Industrial Park, 102 Richard Rd., Ivyland, PA 18974

14. Collins Axe, PO Box 351, Lewiston, PA 17044 (W)

15. Columbia Cutlery Co., PO Box 123, Reading, PA 19603

16. The Cooper Group, PO Box 728, Apex, NC 27502

17. Comet Industries, Div. of Hoffco, Inc., 25 Washington Ave., Richmond, IN 47374 (W)

18. Corona Clipper Co., PO Box 730, Corona, CA 91720

19. Council Tool Co., Inc., PO Box 165, Lake Waccamaw, NC 28450 (W)

20. Echo, Inc., PO Box 578, 3150 MacArthur Blvd. Northbrook, IL 60062 (W)

21. Estwing Mfg. Co., Reading, PA 19603 (W)

22. Fanno Saw Works, PO Box 628, Chico, CA 95926

23. Forestry Suppliers, Inc., Box 8397, Jackson, MS 39204

24. General Supply Corp., Box 9347, Jackson, MS 39206

25. G.F. Hickock, 2344 Stanwell Cir., Concord, CA 94520

26. Homelite, Division of Textron, Inc., PO Box 7047, Charlotte, NC 28217 (W)

27. John Houchins and Sons Co., 400 W. Market St., Newark, NJ 07107 (W)

28. Husquarna, Inc., 224 Thorndale Ave., Bensenville, IL 60106 (W)

29. Jemco Tool Corp., 60 State St., Seneca Falls, NY 13148

30. Johnsons Power Equipment, Rte. 138, Jewett City, CT 06351.

31. Jonsereds AB, Chain Saw Div., S-433 01, Partille, Sweden (W)
32. Kimball Woodcarver Co., 2602 Whitaker St., Savannah, GA 31401
33. Leach Co., PO Box 2608, Oshkosh, WI 54901
34. Leetonia Tool Co., 142 Main St., Leetonia, OH 44431
35. O. P. Link Handle Co., Inc., Norman and Lind Streets, Salem, IN 47167 (W)
36. Maasdam Pow' R-Pull, Inc., 3130 N. Hollywood Way, Burbank, CA 91510
37. Marion Tool Corp., Marion, IN 46952
38. Marlin Industries, 3224 E. Willow St., Long Beach, CA 90806
39. Fred Marvin & Associates, Inc., 1968 Englewood Ave., Akron, OH 44312
40. McCulloch Corp., Los Angeles, CA 90009
41. Ben Meadows Co., Forestry & Engineering Supplies, PO Box 8377, Station F, Atlanta, GA 30306
42. Nelson Paint Co., Box 907, Iron Mountain, MI 49801 (W)
43. New England Handles, PO Box 187, Thompson, CT 06277
44. Oley Tooling, Inc., Oley, PA 19547
45. Owl Brook Distributors, Owl Brook Rd., Ashland, NH 03217 (W)
46. Pennsylvania Saw Corp., 810 Broad St., Newark, NJ 07102 (W)
47. H. K. Porter, Inc., 74 Foley St., Somerville, MA 02143 (W)
48. Rolatape Corp., 1301 Olympic Blvd., Santa Monica, CA 90404 (W)
49. ROWCO Mfg. Co., Inc., 48 Emerald St., Keene, NH 03431
50. Sanal Industrial, Inc., Concord, NH 03301

51. Scott Machine Development Corp., 215 Prospect Ave., Walton, NY 13856
52. Sequatachie Handle Works, Inc., Sequatachie, TN 37374
53. Seymour Smith & Sons, Snap-cut Garden Cutting Tools, Oakville, CT 06779
54. Smith & Hawken Tool Co., 68 Homer, Palo Alto, CA 94301
55. Snow & Nealley Co., 8494 Exchange St., Bangor, ME 04401
56. Southern Coatings and Chemical Co., Inc., Box 160, Sumter, SC 29150 (W)
57. Spencer Industries, Inc., 1508 N. Mascher St., Philadelphia, PA 19122
58. Stanley Tools, Div. of Stanley Works, New Britain, CT 06050 (W)
59. STHIL, Inc., Box 5514, Virginia Beach, VA 23455 (W)
60. The Tufnut Works, 236 Montezuma St., Santa Fe, NM 87501
61. True Temper Corp., 1623 Euclid Ave., Cleveland, OH 44115 (W)
62. TSI Supply Co., PO Box 151, Flanders, NJ 07836
63. Union Fork and Hoe Co., 500 Dublin Ave., Columbus, OH 43216
64. V & B Manufacturing Co., Hebron, IL 60034
65. Voi-Shan, 8463 Higuera St., Box 512, Culver City, CA 90230
66. Wallace Mfg. Corp., 21 Manning Rd., Enfield, CT 06082 (W)
67. The Warwood Tool Co., Wheeling, WV 26003
68. The Warren Group, Div. of Warren Tool Corp., Hiram, OH 44234 (W)
69. Woodcraft Supply Corp., 313 Montvale Ave., Woburn, MA 01801
70. Yankee Mechanics, Inc., RFD 1, Concord, NH 03301

71.  Zip-Penn, Inc., PO Box 179, Erie, PA 16512
72.  Sears and Roebuck
73.  Montgomery Ward & Co.
74.  Antique Stores

_____

(W) Wholesaler

# 13

# DEVELOPING AND USING TRAIL MAINTENANCE INVENTORIES

---

INVENTORIES — OR ASSESSMENTS OF TRAIL conditions and maintenance needs — can prove useful in a variety of ways to trail maintainers, land managers, and others. They can be used for short-term and long-range planning, for scheduling maintenance, for budget preparation, for prioritizing projects, and for guiding trail maintainers in general or specifically assigning them to certain tasks.

### Trail Surveys

Simple trail condition surveys are used to assess gross maintenance needs and to identify some specific trail problems. Most maintainers use them in the spring to prepare for the summer maintenance effort. The AMC trail crew hikes all its trails in the White Mountains in the spring to remove winter blowdowns, clean drainage, and generally identify trail problems; crewmen fill out a "Patroller's Report" (see form A) for each trail. Volunteers performing the same function use a different form (see form B).

*The forms referred to in this chapter appear on pages 231-243.*

The AMC's Boston Chapter utilizes trail maintainers, individual hikers, and trip leaders to provide feedback on trails. Several forms have been prepared for their use (See forms C and D). The Potomac Appalachian Trail Club and Appalachian Trail Conference also have similar forms (See forms E and F). All these assessment forms can be used to collect information on specific problems — e.g., a sign missing — or general maintenance needs — e.g., a boggy or eroded section of trail. Specific problems can be dealt with immediately, while the longer term general problems noted may require a followup field check to thoroughly assess the situation for eventual correction. As can be seen, some forms also provide for opinions on guidebook descriptions, assessment of facilities along the trail, parking accommodations, observations on off-trail or bootleg camping, and other trail-related matters. Some also include sections for reporting work accomplished, if the trip is more than just a survey of conditions.

One should bear in mind that the degree of detail required will vary depending upon the specific questions asked and the trail maintenance experience of the person doing the inventory. Those not well versed in trail problems and solutions to them can be aided through the use of various trail manuals such as this book or the *Appalachian Trail Field Book: A Self-Help Guide For Trail Maintainers* (developed by the Appalachian Trail Conference).

Assessments will be complete or be understated, depending on who is doing the survey. Someone familiar with a trail may not mention sparse blazes, whereas someone on a trail for the first time may have a hard time following it and feel it is underblazed. Also, someone may view a particular gully or other trail problem as standard and not mention it, while someone else might note it as a problem. Therefore, getting input from both maintainers and hikers is ideal, since many and varied opinions can make up for the biases certain to appear if only one or two evaluations are received.

## Work Logs

Detailed inventories of trail maintenance and construction needs, done by one or more people experienced in all aspects of trail work, can also prove useful. Such inventories, or work logs, point out very specific solutions for each trail problem encountered and utilize a reference point system as a guide for trail crews — for assigning specific tasks, prioritizing and scheduling projects, and estimating time and expense required.

Work logs should be prepared by one or more experienced trail people. Two are better than one, since expertise and knowledge can be pooled in evaluating and developing a prescription for a difficult trail problem. Work logs should be done while traveling uphill. More is seen when one is going uphill at a slow pace then when walking downhill, often at a faster pace and when more concerned with footing. Spring is generally the best time to do work logs in most places; then maintainers will pick up water-related problems that will not be seen in late summer or fall.

In terms of equipment, all that is needed is a notebook and pencil, or a cassette recorder or dictaphone, and a measuring wheel of some kind. Do not use ink for field notes unless it is waterproof, since it will become illegible if the paper gets wet. Engineer's fieldbooks with waterproof paper provide perhaps the best writing medium.

Some find a cassette recorder or dictaphone to be faster, easier, and more effective than taking notes; writing can be time-consuming, after all. If developing a work log alone, one can hold a recorder in one hand and the measuring wheel in the other. Otherwise, you have to lay the wheel down or hook it onto your belt in order to free both hands for writing. Also, when writing one tends to abbreviate notations, sometimes leaving out key information in the interest of time — or perhaps ending up with illegible scribbles. You can put in all the detail you wish with a recorder. You just have to make sure the recorder is working properly, and that you bring a battery and extra tapes. Bring a notepad and pencil for emergencies. A clinometer or abney level can be handy for estimating slopes.

Generally, a measuring wheel is used to provide reference points for each work item and distances between items. If measured carefully someone doing the work can rewheel the trail to locate specifically referenced maintenance needs with great accuracy.

Alternatively, one could also develop a permanent trail section grid, placing numbered metal tags, pins, or other markers at certain intervals. The person developing the work log would then list work items as being, for example, between tags 1 and 2, which might be 100 feet apart. In some cases it may not be necessary to do either. A trail could simply be walked and work listed with no reference points (distances) noted or with distances being approximated (see form G). Such a work log, however, may be difficult if not impossible to follow by a trail crew, even though it does provide the types and quantity of work needed on a trail for planning and estimating purposes.

## Using a Work Log

If a trail crew is to do work as outlined specifically in a work log, it can be waterproofed for field use with contact paper. Someone on the crew should ideally help develop the log, so there will be input directly from those who have done and will be doing the work — and also so the crew will understand the work prescriptions and the rationale behind them. Should some-one from the crew not be able to assist the person who does develop the work log, the latter should provide clear work descriptions, give rationales, and cite detailed references. As no work log can ever be considered completely accurate or abso-lutely the best prescription for every trail problem — two logs done by the same person for the same trail at different times will differ — flexible procedures should exist to cope with varia-tions from the work log.

For a trail crew which is inexperienced or for one that is working under contract where only specified work is to be done, flagging tape or wooden stakes can be used to mark each location where work is needed. Either the prescription (e.g., three rock steps) or a reference point keyed to a work log can be placed on the tape or stake, using a permanent marking pen. Reference points are probably best, particularly if the work is scattered, since the crew can correlate the reference point to the work log very easily and quickly. If work prescriptions are only marked on the tape or stake, the crew may become confused about the work to be done at a particular spot in relation to the work log, necessitating backtracking. If flagging or wooden stakes are used, do not place them in the field too long in advance of when the work will be done. Hikers may remove some, thinking they are unaesthetic. Others may simply van-dalize them. When the work is finished, all flagging and stakes should be removed by the crew.

Work logs can also be used as general guides by the trail crew. Work that is low key, low priority, or widely scattered — and that might get overlooked — is more apt to get done when specifically listed.

Supervisors should be aware that requiring a crew to bring a measuring wheel into the woods to locate references and work items can sometimes be undesirable. It may negatively affect the morale of an experienced crew, since they may feel a loss of creative freedom and believe they are locked into estimates made by others. Where a work log is to be used as a guide for an experienced crew, simply put in easily identified natural features as reference points so they can keep track of where they are in the field compared to the work log. This, and possibly some field flagging or staking, will generally eliminate the need for a wheel to be brought into the woods. List all trail junctions, streams, and outlooks. Where work is widely scattered, give a reference such as: ''Need 15' waterbar to left, 10' below large white birch with blaze on right, two big boulders on left just above waterbar location.'' The more detail, the better.

Most work needs will be obvious to an experienced crew, particularly where there is a lot of it in one area. Also, developing a work log with a measuring wheel with five foot increments provides crews with distances that can be easily estimated, paced, and computed without a wheel. Doing a few computations back at the office and placing them on the work log — e.g., the distances between references — helps the crew find things in the field.

Detailed work logs done by experienced trail maintainers can also be invaluable in prioritizing work projects and estimating time and expense involved. Setting priorities can be done by both type and quantity of problems, tying in such factors as use levels and whether or not any work has been done on the trail in the past. A low use trail with a small but severe erosion problem may be of lower priority than a heavily used trail with a long boggy section. Logs which have brief narratives about the nature of the trail sections (e.g., ''gully 3' wide and 1' deep versus 1'' deep'') can also be of help in decision-making. A steep trail with extensive gullies needing one hundred waterbars is probably a higher priority than a trail following an old logging road on a gentle grade that needs one hundred waterbars over its entire length.

To estimate time and expense involved, you must know through regular record-keeping what work has been done by a crew — what amount of work is produced on the average (e.g., fifty bog bridges per four-man crew per week). You can then extrapolate to another trail section. For example, two hundred bridges would probably require four weeks for the crew described above. The cost of the crew per week can be utilized to compute an average cost per work item, which can in turn be used to estimate the cost of completing a large project. A simple tally sheet (see form H) on to which numbers of work items can be placed can facilitate estimating.

Detailed work logs do take time to do. On a trail requiring extensive work, two miles per day might be the average distance covered.

Some people wonder if, because of trail changes over time, detailed work logs might not be quickly outdated. The AMC has found little change overall in tread condition on most trails over a period of 5-10 years, unless use levels change dramatically or a natural catastrophe occurs (e.g., there is a landslide, or a stream jumps its course and floods the trail). A gully noted five years earlier will still be there and probably will not be drastically different. The work prescription should be similar over time, with perhaps only a slightly larger quantity of any one work item to be performed. For planning purposes, work logs should prove to be good for quite a few years. If a crew is to use an old work log as a guide, it should be realized that some field changes will be encountered. Of course, an inexperienced or contract crew should work from an updated work log done the season the work will be performed.

Just as records of what needs to be done on trails can be useful, so also can records of what has been done. Knowing what and when work was done enables the maintainer to gauge the lifespan of various construction and maintenance techniques. Some techniques may be longer lasting than others. Also, by knowing how long work lasts, long-range planning and budgeting for reconstruction can be done. Maintainers can assess the accuracy of their work estimates by comparing original work logs with records of actual construction.

## Form A

AMC TRAIL CREW PATROLLER'S REPORT

Trail: _____Reporter: _____Date: _____
(If Necessary Use Reverse Side For Answers)

I. PRESENT CONDITION OVERALL AND LOCATION
OF PROBLEMS (mud, erosion, etc.):

_____

_____

_____

_____

II. WHAT CONSTRUCTION IS NEEDED? (waterbars,
steps, bridges, cairns, cribbing, etc.):

_____

_____

_____

_____

III. HOW IS EXISTING CONSTRUCTION HOLDING UP?
(if there is any):

_____

_____

_____

_____

IV. DOES THE TRAIL NEED STANDARDIZING? IF SO,
WHERE? IF NOT, THEN WHEN?:

_____

_____

_____

_____

V. ANY MISSING SIGNS OR ONES THAT ARE IN
POOR CONDITION (hard to read or falling apart)?
IS THE TRAIL PAINT BLAZED? WHAT COLOR?
VERY SPORADIC OR EVENLY DONE? CLEAR OR

FADED? ARE THERE SECTIONS OF CONFUSING
TRAIL WHICH REQUIRE BLAZING OR SIGNS?:

_____

_____

_____

_____

VI. OTHER COMMENTS (aesthetic value, long range
proposals):

_____

_____

_____

VII. IF THERE ARE BRIDGES (e.g., suspension bridges or
timber bridges) WHAT ARE THEIR CONDITION?
ARE REPAIRS NEEDED? (steps, railings, floor
boards, creosote)?:

_____

_____

_____

_____

## Form B

### APPALACHIAN MOUNTAIN CLUB WHITE MOUNTAINS VOLUNTEER MAINTAINER WORK TRIP REPORT

Please complete this report after each work trip and forward to your regional overseer.

Volunteer Maintainer _____

Date Report Prepared _____    Date of Work Trip _____

Trail or Section Assignment _____

Briefly describe what basic maintenance work (brushing, blazing, cairns, cleaning of drainage, blowdown removal) was done and approximate location.

_____

_____

_____

_____

_____

Size of work party ____ Approximate number of man-hours ____

What basic maintenance needs did you observe that still need attention? Give approximate location.

_____

_____

_____

_____

_____

Have you observed major maintenance needs? What type and where? New construction or reconstruction/replacement of old work? Can you do any of it? Need trail crew or volunteers?

_____

_____

_____

_____

Any special problems noted, e.g., sign missing or damaged, major bridge repairs? Where?

_____

_____

_____

Any observed needs/problems at any AMC shelters or campsites?

_____

_____

_____

_____

Additional comments: (use reverse side if necessary)

**Form C**

BOSTON CHAPTER AMC
TRAIL INFORMATION
Report by: _____
Address: _____
_____
_____
Date: _____

1  Trail identification: _____ Miles long _____
   Kind of trail — Hiking _____, Nature _____, Canoe _____,
   Ski touring _____, Bicycle _____, Other _____
2  Date of latest hike on trail: _____
3  Towns in which located: _____
4  Terminal location(s): _____
5  Is there a map showing the trail? _____
   Is there a detailed description?_____
   Where can they be found? _____
   If not available otherwise, can you please provide? _____
6  _____ miles of private woods, _____ miles of private fields,
   _____ miles of public woods, _____ fields, _____ streets
   (Best shown on a map.)
7  Are there camping areas? _____, Toilets? _____,
   Shelters? _____
   Describe and give location(s). _____
8  Will you provide update (or new description) for next
   guidebook revision? _____
   If not, whom do you recommend? _____
9  Condition of the trail: _____ Well worn
                       _____ Slightly worn
                       _____ Overgrown
                       _____ Difficult brook crossing

_____ Badly eroded spots
_____ Trail bike bogs
_____ Other? Describe.

10  What kind of marking? _____
    Condition of the marking? _____

11  What maintenance is required now? Blowdowns _____,
    Erosion _____, Overgrowth _____, Other _____
    Who maintains the trail? _____
    If you do, would you like help? _____

12  Status of permission to cross private land?
    _____ Written _____ Recent verbal
    _____ Vague past history _____ Other, describe

13  Is there need for rerouting part of trail?
    Please describe why and how. Will you do it _____ ?
    Do you need help? _____ In what way? _____

14  Do you see the possibilty of extending the trail? And maybe
    joining up with another trail to enlarge the trail network?
    Please give details, including the problems you see, such as
    permission on private land, stream crossing, etc. _____

Please mail to:


## USE BACK OF THIS FORM OR SEPARATE SHEETS
## FOR ADDITIONAL INFORMATION

**Form D**

## BOSTON CHAPTER AMC
## TRAIL INFORMATION

Report by: _____

Address: _____

_____

_____

Date: _____

1 Trail identification: _____ Miles long _____
  Kind of trail — Hiking _____, Nature _____, Ski touring
  _____, Canoe _____, Bicycle _____, Other _____
2 Towns in which located? _____
3 Is there a map showing the trail? _____
  Is there a detailed description? _____
4 Will you provide update (or new description) for next Mass/
  RI Guidebook revision? _____
  If not, whom do you recommend? _____
5 Condition of the trail: _____
6 What maintenance is required? Blowdowns _____,
  Erosion _____, Overgrowth _____, Rerouting? _____
  Who maintains the trail? _____
  If you do, would you like help? _____
7 Do you see the possibility of extending the trail? And maybe
  joining up with another trail to enlarge the trail network?
  Please give details, including the problems you see, such as
  permission on private land, stream crossing, etc. _____

_____

Please mail to:

**Form E**

---

### TRAIL INSPECTION REPORT
### POTOMAC APPALACHIAN TRAIL CLUB

Be specific in describing and locating problems. Example: 4-foot windfall in first mile, or 25 minutes from start, or between second or third stream crossings. Send to PATC. (This self-addressed form may be folded and mailed without an envelope.)

Trail name: _____

Date of inspection: _____, 19_____

Portion of trail covered: (from ? to ?) _____

Paint blazes: (distinct? sufficient? double blazing adequate?) _

_____

Signs: (adequate at crossings and junctions? cairns needed?) ___

_____

Major obstacles: (causing traffic to be diverted or stopped?) ___

_____

Vegetation in trail: (grubbing, trimming or weeding needed?) _

_____

Erosion and water control: (serious loss of trail tread? perennial wetness?) _____

_____

_____

Other: (fire rings, short cutting, litter, vandalism, trespass, trail access, trailhead parking problems, map or guidebook errors or changes, sign changes, shelter problems?)

_____

_____

_____

Trail Inspector: _____ Date: _____, 19____

**Form F**

## APPALACHIAN TRAIL CONDITION EVALUATION

Trail Section: _____

Mileage: _____ Date: _____ Club: _____

Maintainer: _____

NOTE: For help in evaluating and describing the general condition of each kind of trail maintenance, refer to the *A.T. Fieldbook*.

TRAIL CLEARING
General Condition:

Work Needed:

Man-Hours Required:

- - - - - - - - - - - - - - - - - - - - - - - - - - - - - - -

BLAZES, METAL MARKERS
General Condition:

Work Needed:

Man-Hours Required:

- - - - - - - - - - - - - - - - - - - - - - - - - - - - - - -

CAIRNS AND POSTS
General Condition:

Work Needed:

Man-Hours Required:

- - - - - - - - - - - - - - - - - - - - - - - - - - - - - - -

SIGNING
General Condition:

Number to be Erected or Replaced:

Man-Hours Required:

---

TREADWAY STABILITY (EROSION CONTROL)
General Condition:

Work Needed (yards, e.g., 300 yds.):

Man-Hours Required:

---

TREADWAY DRYNESS (DRAINAGE)
General Condition:

Work Needed (yards, e.g., 250 yds.):

Man-Hours Required:

---

TRAILHEADS
General Condition:

Work Needed:

Man-Hours Required:

---

BRIDGES AND STILES
General Condition:

Number to be Erected or Repaired:

Man-Hours Required:

---

---

LITTER
General Condition:

Work Needed:

Man-Hours Required:

_ _ _ _ _ _ _ _ _ _ _ _ _ _ _ _ _ _ _ _ _ _ _ _ _ _ _ _ _ _ _ _ _ _ _ _

WORK COMPLETED
Section: _____
Date: _____
Maintainers: _____
_____

Describe Work Done:

Man-Hours Expended:

Return this evaluation to your Club President, Trails Supervisor, or Committee Chairman.

Extra copies of this form may be obtained from the Appalachian Trail Conference, P.O. Box 236, Harpers Ferry, WV 25425 (304-535-6331).

**Form G**

---

SAMPLE WORK LOG ENTRY
Avalon Trail
6/10/80
by Reuben Rajala


Begin at Crawford Notch, trailhead sign.
First 100 feet flat, no problems.
Next 100 yards — 2% grade, need 3-5
waterbars, scattered throughout.
Next 50 feet — steep, 10% grade, need 10-15
rock steps, 2-3 waterbars.
Trail levels out, sidehill route for ¼ mile, ok.

(No wheel used; simply estimating distances and not pinpoint-
ing work items to specific locations.)

---

## Form H

| REFERENCE POINTS | ROCK STEPS | LOG STEPS | STEP STONES | CRIBBING | WATERBARS | DITCH | TRAIL HEAD | PUNCHEON | CAIRNS | TRAIL CLEARING |
|---|---|---|---|---|---|---|---|---|---|---|
| | | | | | | | | | | |
| | | | | | | | | | | |
| | | | | | | | | | | |
| | | | | | | | | | | |
| | | | | | | | | | | |
| | | | | | | | | | | |
| | | | | | | | | | | |
| | | | | | | | | | | |
| | | | | | | | | | | |
| | | | | | | | | | | |
| | | | | | | | | | | |
| SUB TOTAL | | | | | | | | | | |

**WORK LOG TALLY SHEET**

Location: _____

Done By: _____

Date: _____

Page _____

**14**

# TRAIL DESIGN ON PRIVATE LAND

---

ABOUT TWO-THIRDS OF ALL HIKING IN THE United States takes place on state, county, and private land[1]. Of this, private land will be the most important area for future trail development. Crowded public properties will soon reach a saturation point that will require corresponding development of hiking trails in the private sector if opportunities for hiking are going to keep pace with growing demands.

This trail development on private land is a great challenge because in addition to the requirements for satisfactory hiking and the design considerations relative to soils, topography, and vegetation, the designer must satisfy the demanding and varied requirements that landowners will make conditional to use of their properties.

Trail development on privately owned local property provides recreational opportunities near home. Town and county

---

[1]Lucas, Robert C. and Robert P. Rinehart, "The Neglected Hiker," *Backpacker 13*.

parks become more available to the general citizenry if access is enhanced with trail development, and residents gain recreational opportunities normally reserved for vacation times and places removed from their day-to-day community environment.

Environmental education can be an important trail function, especially at the local level where the school curriculum can be developed to take advantage of nature study that is available with local trail development.

In addition to the obvious recreational value of trails on private land, there are many conservation and land use values which may follow from a successful trail installation. Trails connecting conservation districts add continuity to public protection efforts. By channeling people sensitive to environmental quality through the landscape, trails help to protect land by building a protection-oriented constituency. The environmental considerations of trail design require, by their very nature, the documentation, cataloguing, and use of lands having high natural amenity. Exercises in trail layout in the private sector are exercises in continuous connection of open space property.

This chapter describes the different kinds of landowners and their general concerns with trail use on their property. Techniques for determining ownership and for negotiating with owners are outlined. This information is presented with the idea that the organization sponsoring the trail is trying to secure a legally binding right-of-way from owners in order to guarantee protection of the trail environment in the future.

## Determining Ownerships in a Proposed Trail Corridor

After an initial documentation of trail needs is done and a decision is made to proceed, investigation of ownerships should then be carried out. In order to maintain flexibility that will be needed in negotiating with owners, a broad trail corridor including alternate trail locations should be outlined during the initial stages of planning.

Following is an outline for researching landowners[2]:

1. Obtain access to town tax maps if they exist. If so, they are usually kept by the Assessor's Office or the Town Clerk. The maps are public information and are available for anyone to examine. The information is quite complete, although the boundary lines are not always accurate and do not claim to be so. However, they are close enough for this state of the project. The owners' names, addresses, and acreage are given, and any easements over the property should be marked.

2. Research deeds in the county Registry of Deeds. In addition to checking names and addresses, it is important to look for any easements or restrictions which might already apply to the property. If the town has no tax maps, the process is far more complex, a bit like doing a jigsaw puzzle. Following are some suggested methods:

   a) Ask local residents, generally those who are sympathetic to the trail project, for general landownership patterns, specific owners if known, and ideas on who would be most favorably inclined toward the idea of a trail and land preservation. Find out who else would know landowners and, if necessary, ask for an introduction. Local

---

[2]Kittredge, Lucia, in an unpublished work on the Monadnock-Sunapee Greenway project, sponsored by the Society for the Protection of New Hampshire Forests, Concord, NH, 1974.

residents are probably the most useful sources of information because they are familiar with the use of land over time, attitudes toward conservation, financial status of individual owners, and future plans for the region.

b) Talk to town Selectmen. If supportive of the idea, they are a good source, often knowing from memory who owns what land. The Selectmen's Office should have complete lists of property owners within the town, together with acreage, addresses, and taxes paid. (However, they may have no maps showing boundaries.) They also can give an idea of how much land is being sold in the town, what the various land uses are, and what future plans might affect the trail. It is a good idea to maintain a good working relationship with the town Selectmen, as they may be useful when actually talking with landowners.

c) Talk with surveyors who have surveyed land in the area. Often a few surveyors have been working a region for a number of years and know the land and landowners well, particularly with regard to the larger landholdings. They are a good source of information on existing woods roads, current use of the land, and outstanding natural features, and their familiarity with landowners makes them a likely contact when landowners are approached.

d) Conservation officers of state Fish and Game Departments, county foresters, and consultants from the Soil Conservation Service are another source of information. Often they know a particular area well and can recommend certain landowners who would be more favorably inclined to the project than others. Their greatest help, however, is in knowing the land and its features.

e) The chairpersons of town Conservation Commissions are extremely helpful in most cases, especially since they are sensitive to the conservation attitudes prevalent in the town. Again, they can be most useful when actually contacting landowners.

## Types and Patterns of Ownership

The types and patterns of ownership play an important role in the design and layout of a trail. Studying overall types and patterns of landownership helps to describe the path of least resistance, and therefore the easiest and most economical direction for the trail to follow.

1. **Corporate Owners — Pulp and Paper Companies, Agricultural Ownerships** — Lands held by corporations for timber harvesting and agriculture can be ideal for trail use. Well-planned trail use can be easily adapted to the management programs of these ownerships. The typically large size of forest ownerships lessens the degree of negotiation required of the trail designer per unit of trail mileage gained.

These lands are not disrupted by trail use in the same way residential land would be, being agricultural in nature. Hikers are less aggravating to absentee owners than they are to residential owners who confront the use directly.

Corporate owners make virtually all management decisions on the basis of the financial benefits that accrue to the company's shareholders. Their posture is predictable and consistent; they demonstrate the preeminent practicality of the business establishment. In this light, they are leery of any legal encumbrances that might follow a successful and popular trail installation.

In order to successfully approach these owners with a trail proposal, the designer must have prepared management plans acknowledging their concerns. These concerns generally are oriented around how the trail will foreclose future owner options. Enthusiastic use by the public would make closure a bad public relations issue; accidents could pose an unacceptable liability burden on the owner; and, the very real concerns of fire hazard, parking congestion, vandalism, and sanitation problems can make endorsement of trail proposals by these owners difficult.

2.  **Corporate Owners — Developers and Subdividers —** Owners whose purpose is to develop their landholdings are almost always decidedly negative toward proposals for trail use. From their viewpoint, trails unrealistically foreclose their options.

    Development land virtually precludes the possibility of high-quality trail design because of its usually piecemeal character and its tendency to be subdivided into small units. There have been many cases where existing trails were closed because access had been cut off by development. Many informal, unmaintained paths around cities and towns have been effectively closed in recent years by urban sprawl: limited access highways, airports, and the like. Development land sadly, but effectively narrows trail options and the possibility of success for public trail use.

3.  **Residential Owners —** In town and near urban centers, most ownerships are residential — i.e., owners live on or close to their property. These ownerships require closer, more thorough follow-up for trail installation. Owner attitudes are more varied and therefore the design, in order to meet these varied perspectives, becomes more complex.

A conservation-minded owner will be easier to negotiate with because he shares and can understand the social and environmental goals of the proposed trial. Work, therefore, will be facilitated if owner attitudes are documented in the initial research where possible. This way, when the negotiation stage is reached, the most sympathetic owners can be approached first. Endorsement from these owners will help their less sympathetic neighbors to accept the idea of public trail use. Protection of trails on residential land, depending on the situation, can be so complex as to be unrealistic for trail projects over the long term.

## Concerns of Private Landowners

Owner concerns with public trail development, more particularly with any accompanying legally binding arrangement proposed for the property in question, are legitimate. Try to see a trail proposal from the owner's perspective.

1.    **Future Use of the Proposed Trail Property** — The major concern evident in negotiation for protected trail rights-of-way is that of the landowners for maintaining their future options for use of property proposed for the trail. Trails need not be protected with legal agreements; however, without some protection the trail's future cannot be securely guaranteed. Therefore, the negotiator should propose that some minimum distance around the trail be kept free of incompatible developments such as structures and timber harvesting activity. This distance could be anything from eight feet to a quarter of a mile depending on the owner, the financial resources of the trail sponsor, and the value of the proposed trail. Care should be used in negotiating to anticipate the owner's reaction so that the

proposal does not sound unreasonable. The sponsor must temper his negotiations with sound judgments of the owner's attitudes. In initial transactions, it may be best to simply secure a written pledge from the owner to continue to work with the trail sponsor toward installation and eventual protection.

Legal agreements that protect trails, because of their linear nature, easily bisect owner's property into compartments which can place a serious constraint on its use, particularly for smaller owners. The right-of-way agreement should permit motorized crossing of the corridor plus limited use of vehicles along the trail treadway. This concession, plus the latitude to cut timber according to a simple prescription, offers the possibility of some protection to the trail while giving the owner the freedom he feels is essential in the management of his lands.

The legally binding agreement may require a commitment too great for the owner to accept. The small owner's desire to adapt his land program to changing conditions in his personal or family life or, in the case of corporate owners, the need for latitude to make decisions based on market changes, are highly valued and constitutionally guaranteed freedoms.

If this degree of protection is not possible on a trail route for which no alternatives exist, then the agreement should be adapted to the owner's conditions. In many cases the owner's plans preclude trail development altogether. If this is the case, then not too much can be done to change the situation. Alternative routes must be found.

Of course, a policy of requesting less commitment from owners makes installation easier. In some cases the best course of action may be to simply get verbal, or better, written permission from the owner. This may be the best approach with reticent owners. After careful installation and high-caliber maintenance work geared to winning the owner's support, a gradual program of increasing protective efforts may be more feasible. The practice of the past, of just getting verbal permission for trail use, will diminish in importance in the future. The tenuous status of most trails on private land must be fortified with viable agreements to protect and perpetuate these facilities. If they are not protected, developments will further reduce satisfactory hiking opportunities in the future.

2. **Landowner Concerns — Liability for Hiker Injury** — A second major concern owners frequently have is that they would, by giving approval to the proposed trail, be tacitly accepting an unreasonable degree of liability for accidents that hikers may have on their property.

Inherent in our whole concept of private land is the owner's right to control his land. Because of this control posture the courts have historically held that the owner can prevent hazardous conditions or give warning of hazardous conditions to users of his land. Failures to provide this protection of visitors could be construed by the courts as negligence, which would be the first step in any legal proceedings against a landowner by an injured hiker.

Proving negligence on the part of a landowner requires four elements[3]:
1. Duty or obligation recognized by law requires the owner to conform to a certain standard of conduct for the protection of others against unreasonable risk.

---

[3]Harrington, Robert F., "Liability Exposure in Operation of Recreation Facilities," *Outdoor Recreation Action*, No. 35, Spring, 1975, pp. 22-25.

2.  The failure on the owner's part to conform to the standard required.
3.  A reasonably close causal connection between the conduct and the resulting injury (proximate cause).
4.  Actual loss or damage resulting to the hiker's interest.

3.  **Extent of Duty — The Legal Obligation of the Owner** — Identification of the extent of duty is important because, as indicated in the outline of requirements for negligence, liability is predicated upon one's breach of duty owed to another.[4] This extent of duty owed by an owner to users of his land depends upon the legal status of the person using that land. The legal status of users of land can be divided into three broad categories: (1) trespassers, (2) licensees, and (3) invitees.

The duty of landowners is different for each of these three categories. This sliding scale of legal obligation increases as the status of the visitor increases from trespasser to licensee or from licensee to invitee.

The lowest in this legal scale is the trespasser, defined as "a person who enters upon land without a privilege to do so."[5] The owner owes no duty to the trespasser to use reasonable care to keep his lands safe for him.

There is an important exception to this rule. If the trespasser is a child, the degree of obligation increases. Because of the immaturity of the child, personal judgments on the degree of risk cannot be made. The "attractive nuisance" doctrine grew out of this theory. For instance, if

---

[4]*Ibid.*, p. 22.

[5]*Ibid.*, p. 23.

a mine shaft or well is left uncapped and a child trespasser is injured, the owner may be held liable for a breach of duty owed to the child.

The lowest category of persons entitled to use land is the licensee, which is defined as a person who has been given permission to use land with no benefit of the use going to the owner. In most cases, hikers are given the status of licensee. The hiker comes for his own purpose rather than for any purpose of the owner. If he came without a license he would be a trespasser. The landowner, by giving permission, does *not* extend any assurances that the premises are safe for the purpose for which permission is granted.[6] The duty owed by an owner to a licensee is a negative one. The owner must refrain from malicious and willful failure to warn of or guard against an unseen hazard he knows about. He owes no duty to inspect the premises for safety, nor does he have to warn of hazards that should be obvious to the licensee.

Persons who enter premises for business in which the owner is concerned are given the status of invitees. The historical test of invitee status is whether the owner receives benefit, financial or otherwise, from the person using his land. If a benefit flows to the owner, as would be the case with an entrance fee, then the user would be an invitee. The duty or legal obligation of the owner to an invitee is much greater than the duty owed a licensee. This duty owed is an affirmative one. Not only must the owner protect the invitee from hazards he knows about, but he must also protect him against hazards that he, with reasonable care, might discover in inspecting his land.

---

[6]*Ibid.*, p. 23.

Financial benefits or benefits in kind are the historical test of invitee status. A newer, more nebulous test, called the invitation test, considers the fact that public trails, open for the purpose of public use, invite use and therefore initiate an invitee status on the user. Opening land to the public implies that it has been prepared for their reception.[7] This theory is being upheld in more and more recent court cases.

The liability of landowners then, in cases other than malicious or willful failure to warn, is a function of the status of use applied to the person using the land.

It seems clear that the hiker is a licensee and as such accepts the risks of his activities as his own. However, to date there has not been enough litigation to supply the precedential standards upon which the distinction between licensee and invitee can be finally and clearly made for all situations. It seems likely that the courts will enforce greater responsibility on owners in the future because of a generally increasing concern for safety, evident in the consumer movement and in other developing attitudes in our society.

## State Laws

Thirty-eight out of forty-seven states in the United States that responded to a survey conducted by the Trails Advisory Committee of Rhode Island[8] have laws whose purpose is to limit the liability of owners who open their land to passive recreational use such as hiking. These laws help to ensure that the duty of

[7]*Ibid.*, p. 24.

[8]Rhode Island State Trail Advisory Committee, *Report of the Trail Advisory Committee*, State of Rhode Island and Bureau of Outdoor Recreation, November, 1974, p. 13.

owners is the duty owed to a licensee. Lack of court cases, however, has precluded a viable test of these laws. It can be presumed, though, that such laws help to keep the legal obligation of owners at an acceptable level, and that therefore they can be used to inform owners of the limits of the legal risks they will probably incur with public trail use.

These laws help keep liability insurance premiums at a fairly low cost, which consequently makes feasible the purchase of insurance to add protection to landowners who open their lands to recreational use.

Indemnification of landowners by the trail clubs responsible can be tried. However, this should only be done on a case-by-case basis, and then only after a qualified legal opinion has been obtained.

## Insurance[9]

The purpose of insurance is to spread risk over a population large enough so that no insured party would suffer unacceptable losses in the event of a mishap. Insurance is available to private landowners concerned with the liability they may incur by opening land to hiking.

Most landowners have homeowner's insurance policies which adequately cover their risks. However, if not or if additional coverage is deemed necessary, it might best be purchased by the trail sponsor.

In seeking proper insurance, a local agent is usually in the best position to know a landowner's needs. It is important that

[9]Bureau of Outdoor Recreation, *Liability and Insurance Protection for Private Recreation Enterprises.*

this agent understand the nature of the recreational program as well as the volume of recreational use and potential hazards. State laws limiting landowner liability should be brought to the attention of the agent.

Because the insurance market for private recreation facilities is relatively new, it behooves the trail sponsor or owner to seek rates from several companies before making a final choice. Liability insurance covers losses up to policy limits suffered by the owner as a result of a successful lawsuit by an injured hiker. The policy may cover expenses for medical treatment and rescue at the scene of the mishap. It may also cover investigation, defense, and settlement costs.

There are two basic types of liability insurance policies available to managers of recreation facilities on private land: the Owner, Landlord, and Tenant Policy (OL&T) and the Comprehensive General Liability Policy.

The OL&T policy is the basic way for covering legal liability to the public. Campgrounds and parking areas may be covered under this type of policy.

In the past, many insurance companies have recommended coverage limits of $25,000 per person, $50,000 per accident, and $10,000 in property damages (25/50/10), but because of the increasing amount of court awards and liability claim settlements higher limits should be considered.

The Comprehensive General Liability Policy offers extensive coverage unless specific risks are excluded. Its major advantage for trail use is that it covers almost all hazards.

## Overuse, Vandalism, Parking, and Other Management Problems

If the owner's reservations regarding future use and liability are quelled, concerns over the actual management of the proposed trail may become the greatest cause for reticence in an owner's support. All of the problems that can develop on public trails can develop on trails in the private sector. These problems range from physical deterioration of soils through erosion to the social problems of overcrowding, vandalism, parking congestion, and littering. These problems and their attendant solutions are described in other portions of this book; therefore, there is no need to describe them here. A responsible trail organization will make the point to owners that problems have solutions and that these problems will be controlled using proven management techniques.

The basic point, then, is to impart knowledge to the owner and inspire trust in him for the maintenance organization that will be responsible for the trail. It is presumed that the sponsoring organization will have made judgments on its own capabilities to meet this responsbility. This is imperative before winning landowner support for, if management tasks exceed capabilities and problems develop, then the owner's trust in the organization will be diminished.

A safe procedure for new trails is to initially limit information on the trail's availability. Management problems are almost directly proportional to the volume of use a trail receives. If the information on a trail is limited, then so is use. Gradually increasing trail information and its subsequent use can give the trail manager the staggered start he needs to increase his management profile with increasing use. In this way problems can be solved at an early stage and not after they become full-blown irritants to the owner. The capability of the maintaining organization will obviously not be as heavily taxed on a trail with low or moderate public use.

## Protection of Trails on Private Land

The development and utilization of land protection devices for trail corridors is still a technique that is in the infant stage of development. It is a vast subject that at some stage usually requires legal counsel, considerable expense, and time-consuming negotiations. This book can contain only a cursory review of some of the available mechanisms and their benefits and drawbacks when applied to trails.

"A primary concern in initiating an effort to protect a trail is that all persons involved have complete and uniform understanding of the project involved, methods of accomplishing it, and how it is to function and be administered."[10] If policies and modes of implementation are not clearly understood and collectively acknowledged, then negotiations for agreements will not occur.

Skill and enthusiasm on the part of the person carrying out the negotiations with owners is a critical element of success. Likewise, a good public relations profile in the proposed trail region can pave the way to the owner's door. In public relations it is again imperative to stress that the policies underlying implementation of the project be clearly understood. Conflicting information will sow seeds of distrust and reticence in landowners.

It is also imperative that the negotiator be thoroughly familiar

---

[10]Platt, Rutherford, *National Symposium on Trails*, Washington, DC, June 2-6, 1971, p. 94.

with the characteristics of the land on which the trail is proposed. Before approaching an owner, the negotiator should have information on the owner's perspectives and views on trail use. This will greatly facilitate the development of a successful approach to him. It will also help to develop a protective device that best suits his individual needs.

The largest, most sympathetic, and most influential owners should be approached first. Owners who seem less supportive can be approached after endorsement from their neighbors is assured.

Although individual adaptations of the trail arrangement for each owner can be made, every owner should have the feeling of being treated equally. If special accommodations are made for one, then dissatisfaction may reign among neighboring owners.

A low key, soft sell approach reduces the likelihood that an owner will feel threatened. This is especially important in these modern times when the demands on the private sector are growing. Owners feel defensive about ownership; the proper approach is essential to overcoming this defensiveness.

A firmness, however, is also called for. Legal agreements that do not bind the owner to conditions perpetuating a high-quality environment for the trail fail to supply the protection that trails desperately need if they are to fulfill their future role.

In establishing a trail right-of-way, there are five legal arrangements that can be made with landowners.[11] These range in legal effect from outright acquisition in fee simple to an

---

[11]Crowthers, Leah, in an unpublished work on the Monadnock-Sunapee Greenway project, sponsored by the Society for the Protection of New Hampshire Forests, Concord, NH, 1974.

informal agreement with an owner. Because a legal contract requires a writing, the oral agreement is not legally enforceable and therefore is clearly not appropriate in a trail project except at the initial stages of planning and installation. A complete transfer of ownership may simply not be financially feasible, nor is it necessary except perhaps where permanent facilities such as parking lots and campsites are provided.

Between the two extremes of oral agreement and ownership in fee, there are three limited legal interests that can be placed on trail corridor land. In order according to the extent of the interest, these are the easement, the lease, and the license. These non-possessory interests in land offer much flexibility and are excellent techniques for realizing private wishes with respect to the land. Each of these arrangements requires a careful consideration of their respective characteristics.

The easement is the strongest of the non-possessory interests in land. The extent of the interest conveyed needs to be explicitly outlined in the Deed of Conveyance, which is recorded in public records of title. It may be limited to a specific duration or may be granted in perpetuity. Nevertheless, it is binding upon all future owners. With the exception of reverter clauses specifying the termination of interest upon the occurrence of certain events, it is not revocable.

The lease involves an interest in land upon the payment of an agreed-upon fee. It has the advantage to the landowner of being a terminable arrangement upon the expiration of a certain period of time, but the power of termination is limited to the terms of the written arrangement.

The third and most limited non-possessory interest in land is the license, which is revocable at the will of either party to the agreement. This is the simplest legal device and the least formidable to the owner, who can rest assured that there is no threat of litigation should he decide that the arrangement is no longer in his best interest. The non-binding character of the license makes it fairly easy to consummate with owners; however, it has obvious limitations to the trail interests it protects.

# FURTHER READING

## Trail Construction

*Adirondack Mountain Club Trail Maintenance Manual* (draft), The Adirondack Mountain Club, Inc., 172 Ridge St., Glens Falls, NY 12801, 23 pages, price unknown.

*The Appalachian Trail Stewardship Manual: Book 1, Trail Design, Construction and Maintenance* (draft), W. Birchard, editor, The Appalachian Trail Conference, Harpers Ferry, WV, 1981, approx. 200 pages, price unknown. An excellent all-around trail manual focusing specifically on the Appalachian Trail; useful on all trails.

*Arkansas Trails System Maintenance Manual*, Arkansas Deparment of Parks & Tourism, Parks Division, One Capital Mall, Little Rock, AK 72201, 46 pages, price 50¢.

*Backpack Trail Maintenance*, U.S. Forest Service, Equipment Development Center, Missoula, MT, 127 pages, free.

*Erosion Control on Logging Roads in the Appalachians,* James Kochenderfer, Northeast Forest Experiment Station, Upper Darby, PA, 1979, 28 pages, free. Useful information on road maintenance which could be applicable for hiking, ski touring, and horse trails that use roadbeds.

*Field Guide for Routine Recreation Trail Maintenance,* State of Washington, Department of Natural Resources, Recreation Division, Building 17, Olympia, WA 98504, 42 pages, price unknown.

*Florida Trail Manual,* Florida Trails Association, Inc., Box 137008, Gainesville, FL 32604, 30 pages, cost unknown.

*Footpaths in the Countryside,* T. Huxley, Countryside Commission for Scotland, Battleby, Redgorton, Perth PH1 3EW, Scotland, 1975, 51 pages, price unknown. An excellent book on trail construction, maintenance, and management experiences in Scotland and Britain.

*Forest Service Trails Handbook* (FSH 7709.12), U.S. Forest Service. Pretty good rundown of some construction techniques. Western oriented.

*Guide for Mountain Trail Development,* Colorado Mountain Trails Foundation, Inc., Box 2238, Littleton, CO 80161, 120 pages, price unknown.

"Hardwood Bark Chips as a Surfacing Material for Recreation Trails," Robert Holmes, Gerald Coorts, and Paul Roth, *Forest Products Journal,* Vol. 23, No. 5, May, 1975.

*Indiana Trails Construction and Maintenance Manual,* Indiana Division of Outdoor Recreation, Department of Natural Resources, 112 pages, $1.00.

*The Nature and Properties of Soils*, 7th editon, Harry O. Buckman and Nyle C. Brady, Macmillan Company, price unknown.

*Nonmotorized Trails: An Introduction to Planning and Development*. Department of Environmental Resources, Division of Outdoor Recreation, Bureau of State Parks, P.O. Box 1467, Harrisburg, PA 17120, 1980, 71 pages, price unknown. Information on hiking, bicycle, water, horse, and ski touring trails, as well as trails for the handicapped.

*Pacific Crest Trail*, U.S. Department of Agriculture, Forest Service, 14th St. and Jefferson Dr., SW, Washington, DC 20250, 1971, price unknown.

*Practices and Problems in Trail Maintenance and Construction*, U.S. Forest Service, Equipment Development Center, Missoula, MT, 80 pages, price unknown.

*Surfacing Forest Trails with Crushed Rock*, Report #7700-5, U.S. Forest Service, Equipment Development Center, Missoula, MT, 1975, 13 pages, free.

*Trail Construction Manual*, Tennessee Department of Conservation, 2611 West End Ave., Nashville, TN 37203, 46 pages, price unknown.

*Trail Manual for the Appalachian Trail*, 6th edition, Appalachian Trail Conference, Box 326, Harpers Ferry, WV 25425, 1966, $1.00. A manual giving good instructions on layout, cutting, and blazing.

*Trail Planning and Layout,* Audubon Society, Nature Center Planning Division, 950 3rd Ave., New York, NY 10022,

$3.00. Very good on construction and layout of nature trails and other trailside interpretive facilities.

*Trails in Nature Conservancy Preserves,* TNC Stewardship Studies Leaflet #2, Julie Nagazina and Ronald Killian, The Nature Conservancy, 1800 N. Kent St., Arlington, VA 22209, 1980, 43 pages, price unknown.

*Trails Manual,* Charles Vogel, Equestrian Trails, Inc., 10723 Riverside Dr., N. Hollywood, CA 91602, price unknown. A manual oriented to western horse trails. Good presentation of basic drainage requirements.

## State Trail Reports

*Chickasaw Bluffs Master Plan,* Tennessee Department of Conservation, Division of Planning, 2611 West End Ave., Nashville, TN 37203, 1975, 82 pages, price unknown.

*Cumberland Trail Master Plan,* Tennessee Department of Conservation, Division of Planning, 2611 West End Ave., Nashville, TN 37203, 1974, 75 pages, price unknown.

*Hiking and Equestrian Trails in California,* State of California, Department of Parks and Recreation, Box 2390, Sacramento, CA 95811, 95 pages, cost unknown.

*New Hampshire Statewide Trails Study,* State Office of Comprehensive Planning, State House Annex, Concord, NH 03301, 1974, price unknown. This report contains the findings and recommendations of a year-long study of the potential for a Statewide Trails System for New Hampshire.

*North Carolina Trails Committee Annual Report,* Department of Natural and Economic Resources, Raleigh, NC, 1974, price unknown. This first annual report presents a summary of the North Carolina Trails Committee's work and findings for calendar year 1974.

*Report of the Colorado Recreational Trails Committee,* Colorado Division of Parks and Outdoor Recreation, 1973, 32 pages, price unknown. Information on all aspects of trail development, maintenance, and management.

*Report of the Rhode Island Trail Advisory Committee,* Rhode Island Statewide Planning Program, 265 Melrose St., Providence, RI 03907, free. This report discusses opportunities and current problems confronting the Department in the establishment of a trail program and recommends actions to correct these problems.

*Trail Construction Guidelines for Missouri State Parks,* Missouri Department of Natural Resources, Box 176, Jefferson City, MO 65101, 1977, approx. 50 pages, price unknown.

*A Trail Manual for the East Bay Regional Park District,* East Bay Regional Park District, 11500 Skyline Blvd., Oakland, CA 94619, 1976, 71 pages, $2.00. Information on biking, hiking, and equestrian trail development, maintenance, and management.

## Trail Management

*Managing Vandalism: A Guide to Reducing Damage at Parks and Recreation Facilities,* Park Manned Center for Urban Affairs, 33 Beacon St., Boston, MA 02108, 58 pages, price $1.

## Tools

*Crosscut Saw Manual,* Warren Miller, U.S. Department of Agriculture, Forest Service, Equipment and Development Center, Missoula, MT, price unknown.

## Maps/Aerial Photos

National Cartographic Information Center, U.S. Geological Survey, 507 National Center, Reston, VA 22092. Information on cartographic data, multiuse maps, geodetic control, aerial photography, and space imagery. Several brochures are available: "Types of Maps Published by Government Agencies," "Public Inquiries, Topographic Maps," "A Selected Bibliography on Maps and Mapping," "Geologic Maps: Portraits of the Earth," "Topographic Maps: Silent Guides for Outdoorsmen," "Map, Line, and Sinker."

User Services, EROS Data Center, Sioux Falls, SD 57198. Information on imagery and photography of the Earth's surface features from NASA, NASA's LANDSAT program, and other federal agencies and programs.

## Ski Touring

"Building Your Own X-C Trail", Bill Rice, *X-Country Skier Magazine,* November, 1977, pages 35-38.

"Cross Country Skiing", O. A. Christiansen, Parks and Recretion Magazine, February, 1978, pages 46-50.

*Cross-Country Ski Trail and Facility Design Manual,* Ontario Ski Council, 160 Vanderhoof Ave., Toronto, Ontario M4G 4B8, Canada, 1980, 119 pages, $10.00.

*Cross Country Ski Trails: Guide to Their Design and Management,* Paul F. Rasmussen, Gary R. Clay, and Stuart N. Spetzner, Northern Illinois Planning Commission, 400 W. Madison St., Chicago, IL 60606, price unknown.

*Cross Country Ski Trails: A Starter Manual,* Stanton Allaben and Howard Peterson, U.S. Ski Association, Box 777, Brattleboro, VT 05301, 45 pages, price $4.50.

"Cutting a Cross-Country Ski Trail", John P. Wigin, *Country Journal,* January, 1979, pages 45-47.

*Development Criteria for Cross-Country Ski Trails,* State of Minnesota, Department of Natural Resources, Centennial Office Building, Saint Paul, MN 55155, approx. 30 pages, part of a larger agency manual (Chapter 2), price unknown.

*Guide to Vermont Ski Area Trail Construction and Management,* Pamphlet No. 39. Agricultural Experiment Station, University of Vermont, Burlington, VT 05401, price unknown.

*Guidelines for Selecting Trails and Terrain Suitable for Nordic Skiing,* New York State Department of Evironmental Conservation, 50 Wolf Rd., Albany, NY 12233, 6 pages, 1977, part of larger agency manual.

*An Organizer's Manual: Cross Country Citizens Racing,* U.S. Ski Association, Box 777, Brattleboro, VT 05301, 1978, approx. 50 pages, price unknown.

*The Skier Tourer's Manual,* Ski Touring Council, Troy, VT 05068, 1975, price unknown.

*Ski Touring Guide,* 12th edition, Ski Touring Council, Troy, VT 05868, approx. 100 pages, price unknown.

*Ski Trails and Their Own Design,* Charles N. Proctor, AMC, *Appalachia Journal,* June, 1933, pages 427-431.

*Snow Trail Standards Handbook* (draft), U.S. Forest Service, Washington, DC, 1978, approx. 20 pages, price unknown.

*State of Wisconsin Trail Specifications Handbook,* State of Wisconsin, Department of Natural Resources, Madison, WI, approx. 50 pages, price unknown.

*Touring Center Operation Manual,* National Ski Touring Operators Association, Box 557, Brattleboro, VT 05301, approx. 100 pages, 1979, price unknown.

*Trail Manual,* Parks Canada, Ottawa, Canada, 1978, approx. 200 pages, price unknown.

*Trail Manual* (draft), Ministry of National Resources, Parliament Building, Toronto M7A 1W3, 90 pages, 1978. Price unknown.

## Off-Road Vehicles

*Five State Approaches to Trailbike Recreation Facilities and Their Management,* Robert Rasor, American Motorcyclist Association, P.O. Box 141, Westerville, OH 43081, 1977, 64 pages, $3.95. An excellent book, well illustrated, on development, maintenance, and management of trailbike facilities based on experiences in various states; includes information on laws and regulations in each of the states covered.

*Motorized Trails: An Introduction to Planning and Development,* Department of Environmental Resources, Division of Outdoor Recreation, Bureau of State Parks, P.O. Box 1467, Harrisburg, PA 17120, 1980, 50 pages, price unknown. A very good manual on all types of off-road vehicle trails.

*The Off-Road Vehicle and Environmental Quality,* Malcolm F. Baldwin and Dan H. Stoddard, Jr., Conservation Foundation, 1717 Massachusetts Ave., NW, Washington, DC 20036, 1973, $4.00. An updated report on the social and environmental effects of off-road vehicles, particularly snowmobiles, with suggested policies for their control.

U.S. Department of the Interior, *Planning for Trailbike Recreation.* Heritage Conservation and Recreation Service, Washington, DC 20240, 1979, 93 pages, free. This is a compilation of numerous papers delivered at workshops on trailbike planning and management held throughout the country; the workshops were sponsored by the Motorcycle Council and government planning agencies in 1977 and 1978.

*Trails: A Strategy for Snowmobile Fun and Safety,* Snowmobile Safety and Certification Committee, Inc., 1755 Jefferson Davis Highway, Arlington, VA 22202, 1975, price unknown. This draft version has been prepared exclusively for review by governmental officials and other members of the snowmobile community, and as a means to generate further discussion in the important area of winter outdoor recreation facilities.

*Turkey Bay Off-Road Vehicle Area at Land between the Lakes: An Example of New Opportunities for Managers and Riders,* Douglas N. McEwen, American Motorcyclist Association, P.O. Box 141, Westerville, OH 43081, 1978, 28 pages,

$1.50. This is a case history of an off-road recreation area, located in a National Recreation Demonstration Area managed by the Tennessee Valley Authority; it covers planning and management history, as well as use and maintenance.

*Washington Off-Road Vehicle Guide,* Terry Graham, State of Washington, Department of Natural Resources, Public Lands Building, Olympia, WA 98504, 1980, 55 pages, price unknown. More than just a guide, this excellent publication covers state laws and regulations, safety, opportunities for volunteer maintenance, and sources for information on ORV trails and areas throughout the state.

## Private Land/Trail Protection

*The Appalachian Trail: Guidelines for Preservation,* Department of Landscape Architecture, Pennsylvania State University, State College, PA, 1977, 126 pages, price unknown.

*Long Distance Trails: The Appalachian Trail as a Guide to Future Research and Management Needs,* School of Forestry & Environmental Studies, Yale University, New Haven, CT, 160 pages, price $15.

*Incentives to Use of Land for Outdoor Recreation Purposes: Insulation from Tort Liability: Tax Relief,* University of Georgia Law School, Bureau of Outdoor Recreation, Southeast Regional Office, 148 Cain St., Atlanta, GA. A good rundown on the legal liability of landowners who open their lands for recreational uses such as hiking.

*Operations Manual for a Landowner Program,* Richard Galanlowicz, Open Space Institute, 145 East 52nd St., New York, NY 10033, 1971.

**Landowner Liabilities**

*Liability and the Landowner in Vermont,* Darby Bradley, VNRC Environmental Law Service, Vermont Natural Resources Council, 26 State St., Montpelier, VT 05602, 1977, 10 pages, price unknown.

*Private Lands and Public Recreation: A Report and Proposed Model Act on Access, Liability and Trespass,* W. L. Church, National Association of Conservation Districts, P.O. Box 885, League City, TX 77573, 1979, 33 pages, $1.00. A report on the use of private land for recreation, history of landowner liability, and some recent efforts to modify legislation.

*State Statutes Limiting Landowner Liability for Land Used for Recreational Purposes,* Samuel Bufford, American Motorcyclist Association, P.O. Box 141, Westerville, OH 43081, 1977, 67 pages, $5.00. An excellent source of information on landowner liability in general and specifics on laws in each state.

**Land Use Planning**

American Planning Association, 1776 Massachusetts Ave., NW, Washington, DC 20036. Source of many good books and materials on all aspects of land use planning.

*Conservation Easements,* Paul Allen, The Maryland Environmental Trust, 8 East Mulberry St., Baltimore, MD 21202, 1974, 24 pages, price unknown.

*Designed for Recreation,* Elizabeth Beazley, Faber and Faber, 24 Russell Sq., London, England, 1969. Good information on recreational issues, including trails, in Britain.

*A Guide: Using Conservation Deeds to Maintain Open Space Uses,* Society for the Protection of New Hampshire Forests, Concord, NH 03301, 1975, 20 pages, price unknown.

*Guiding Growth and Change: A Handbook for the Massachusetts Citizen,* Sarah Peskin, Appalachian Mountain Club, 5 Joy St., Boston, MA 02108, 1978, 160 pages, $6.95.

*Land Conservation and Preservation Techniques,* Timothy Fox, Heritage Conservation and Recreation Service, U.S. Department of the Interior, Washington, DC 20243, 1979, 79 pages, free.

*Land, the Most Enduring Gift,* George Russell, Connecticut Department of Environmental Protection, State Office Building, Hartford, CT 06115, 21 pages, price unknown.

*Open Space Protection Techniques,* Ron King, Society for the Protection of New Hampshire Forests, Concord, NH 03301, 1974, 35 pages, price unknown.

*Planning for Urban Trails,* Mary E. Brooks, American Society of Planning Officials, 1313 East Sixtieth St., Chicago, IL 60637, 1969, 32 pages, price unknown.

*Private Approaches to the Preservation of Open Land,* Russell Brenneman, The Conservation and Research Foundation, Inc., 13 Woodsea Place, Waterford, CT 06385, price unknown.

*Protecting Nature's Estate: Techniques for Saving Land*, Emily J. Stover, editor, joint project of the Bureau of Outdoor Recreation, The Nature Conservancy, and the New York State Office of Parks and Recreation, Superintendent of Documents, U.S. Government Printing Office, Washington, DC 20402, 123 pages, $3.25.

*Protecting Open Space: A Guide to Selected Protection Techniques*, Elizabeth Kline, Society for the Protection of New Hampshire Forests, Concord, NH 03301, 1975, 83 pages, $2.00.

## Special Trails

*Design Standards to Accomodate People with Physical Disabilities in Park and Open Space Planning*, Michael L. Ries, Recreation Resources Center, University of Wisconsin—Extension, 1815 University Ave., Madison, WI 53706, 1973, 73 pages, price unknown. Discusses general site considerations, vehicle and pedestrian traffic, and specifications for furnishings, buildings and utilities, recreation facilities, and children's play areas.

## Volunteers in Trail Work

*Mountain Trail Volunteers: A Guide to Working Safely*, Colorado Mountain Trails Foundation, Box 2238, Littleton, CO 80122, 1976, 32 pages, price unknown.

*Volunteer Handbook: A Resource Guide on Volunteerism for Park and Recreation and Heritage Conservation Organizations*, Heritage Conservation and Recreation Service, U.S. Department of the Interior, Washington, DC 20240, 1978, 44 pages, price unknown.

*Volunteers in Action,* Sempervirens Fund, P.O. Box 1141, Los Altos, CA 94022, 1980, $5.00.

*Volunteers: The Magic Plus,* New Hampshire Charitable Fund, 1 South State St., Concord, NH 03301, 42 pages, $3.75.

## Other

*American Barns and Covered Bridges,* Eric Sloane, Wilfred Funk, Inc., 1954.

*Covered Bridges of the Northeast,* Richard Allen, Stephen Greene Press, 1974.

Both have some general information on kingpost, queenpost, and other wooden truss bridges.

*Equipment Tips: Trails Equipment Publications and Films,* U.S. Forest Service, Equipment Development Center, Missoula, MT.

*The Forgotten Art of Building a Stone Wall,* Curtis Fields, Yankee, Inc., Dublin, NH, 61 pages, $2.50. Some good information on use and moving of rock for stone wall construction; applicable to some trail work techniques.

*Hiking and Hiking Trails: A Trails and Trails Based Activities Bibliography,* Mary E. Barkauskas, Bibliography Series #20, Office of Library Services, U.S. Department of the Interior, Washington, DC 20240, 1970, 57 pages, price unknown.

*Log Bridge Construction Handbook,* M. Nagy, J. Trebett, and G. Wellburn, Forest Engineering Research Institute of

Canada, 2010-2112 West Broadway, Vancouver, BC V6K 2C8 Canada, 1980, 421 pages, $25.00. Focusing on bridge construction for logging roads, this book has much technical and practical information on bridge building that could be scaled down for hiking or ski trail use.

*Recreation Trails in Canada: A Comment and Bibliography on Trail Development and Use with Special Reference to the Rocky Mountain National Parks and Proposed Great Divide Trail,* John S. Marsh, Council of Planning Libraries, P.O. Box 229, Monticello, IL 61856, 1971, 17 pages, $2.00.

*Trails Slide Program,* Trails Unlimited, 2134 Montecito Ave., Santa Rosa, CA 95404.

# INDEX

Introductory matter, individual tool suppliers not mentioned in the text but listed on pages 216-222, and sources cited in the footnotes and bibliography have not been indexed. Index citations in italics refer to illustrations.

## ABOUT THE A.M.C.

The Appalachian Mountain Club is a non-profit volunteer organization of over 25,000 members. Centered in the northeastern United States with headquarters in Boston, its membership is worldwide. The A.M.C. was founded in 1876, making it the oldest and largest organization of its kind in America. Its existence has been committed to conserving, developing, and managing dispersed outdoor recreational opportunities for the public in the Northeast and its efforts in the past have endowed it with a significant public trust and its volunteers and staff today maintain that tradition.

Ten regional chapters from Maine to Pennsylvania, some sixty committees, and hundreds of volunteers supported by a dedicated professional staff join in administering the Club's wide-ranging programs. Besides volunteer organized and led expeditions, these include research, backcountry management, trail and shelter construction and maintenance, conservation, and outdoor education. The Club operates a unique system of eight alpine huts in the White Mountains, a base camp and public information center at Pinkham Notch, New Hampshire, a new public service facility in the Catskill Mountains of New York, five full service camps, four self-service camps, and nine campgrounds, all open to the public. Its Boston headquarters houses not only a public information center but also the largest mountaineering library and research facility in the U.S. The Club also conducts leadership workshops, mountain search and rescue, and a youth opportunity program for disadvantaged urban young people. The A.M.C. publishes guidebooks, maps, and America's oldest mountaineering journal *Appalachia*.

*We invite you to join and share in the benefits of membership.* Membership brings a subscription to the monthly bulletin *Appalachia;* discounts on publications and at the huts and camps managed by the Club; notices of trips and programs; and, association with chapters and their meetings and activities. Most important, membership offers the opportunity to support and share in the major public service efforts of the Club.

Membership is open to the general public upon completion of an application form and payment of an initiation fee and annual dues. Information on membership as well as the names and addresses of the secretaries of local chapters may be obtained by writing to: The Appalachian Mountain Club, 5 Joy Street, Boston Massachusetts 02108, or calling during business hours 617-523-0636.